"Is knowing the heart of God the hope of your heart? *I Am* will not only unveil fresh vistas of God's character and ways, but will take you behind the veil into a deeper encounter with him. And, after all, is this not the core of the revival the whole church is praying for?"

DAVID BRYANT, PRESIDENT,
CONCERTS OF PRAYER INTERNATIONAL
CHAIRMAN, AMERICA'S NATIONAL PRAYER COMMITTEE

"*I am* taking special delight in the depth of the message that Steve's writings are bringing to the church."

PASTOR JACK HAYFORD,
THE CHURCH ON THE WAY, VAN NUYS, CALIFORNIA

"*I Am* renewed my hunger to know God. With insight that comes from hiding away with the Master and with the humility and honesty of a fellow pilgrim, Steve Fry encourages us to pursue intimacy with God. The chapter on 'God's Silence' is worth the whole book."

STEVE GREEN, CHRISTIAN ARTIST,
AUTHOR OF *THE POWER OF THE CROSS*

"Steve Fry has been wonderfully used of God to give a very special gift to those who long to know God more intimately and enjoy him more fully. This is a book that will challenge, inform, bless, and enable all those who want to draw nearer to our Lord and live in deeper communion with him."

DR. PAUL A. CEDAR,
CHAIRMAN, MISSION AMERICA

"Steve Fry is an essential gift to our generation. His message leads me straight into the presence of my heavenly Father."

JOHN DAWSON, FOUNDER/DIRECTOR,
INTERNATIONAL RECONCILIATION COALITION
AUTHOR OF *TAKING OUR CITIES FOR GOD*

"[*I Am* is] a devotional kaleidoscope. With each turn of the page, a new and dazzling facet of God's character tumbles into view."

"As I have turned the pages of this incredible book, I have met with God time and time again. Somehow Steve Fry has an ability to touch the deepest part of the human heart and connect it to God. I love this book! It will change your life!"

I Am

THE UNVEILING
OF GOD

STEVE FRY

Multnomah Publishers® *Sisters, Oregon*

I AM

Published by Multnomah Publishers, Inc.

© 2000 by Steve Fry

International Standard Book Number 1-57673-690-3

Cover design by Chris Gilbert
Cover image by JD Marston Photography

The Holy Bible, New International Version (NIV)
© 1973, 1984 by International Bible Society,
used by permission of Zondervan Publishing House

Also quoted:
The Holy Bible, King James Version (KJV)
New Revised Standard Version Bible (NRSV)
© 1989 by the Division of Christian Education
of the National Council of the Churches of Christ
in the United States of America
The Good News Bible: The Bible in Today's English Version (TEV)
© 1976 by American Bible Society
Multnomah is a trademark of Multnomah Publishers, Inc.,
and is registered in the U.S. Patent and Trademark Office.
The colophon is a trademark of Multnomah Publishers, Inc.

Printed in the United States of America

For information:
MULTNOMAH PUBLISHERS, INC.•P.O. BOX 1720•SISTERS, OR 97759

Library of Congress Cataloging-in-Publication Data:

Fry, Steve.
    I AM: The Unveiling of God/by Steve Fry.
    p. cm.
    ISBN 1-57673-690-3 (alk. paper)
    1. Spiritual life—Christianity. I. Title.
BV4501.2.F787 2000
242 21; aa05 12-01—dc99   99-059105

00 01 02 03 04 05 – 6 5 4 3 2 1 0

I want to dedicate this to my mom, Peggy, under whose nurture I learned so many of the ways of God. Hers has been the hand that has steadied me through crisis after crisis; hers the words that have comforted me when it seemed my world was collapsing; hers the counsel that has spared me from more than one disaster.

Mine is a son's debt of never-ending joy to a mother of never-ending faith.

"I AM WHO I AM."
EXODUS 3:14

❧

"Anyone who has seen me has seen the Father."
JOHN 14:9

❧

"In the beginning you laid the
foundations of the earth,
and the heavens are the work of
your hands.
They will perish, but you remain;
they will all wear out like a garment.
Like clothing you will change them
and they will be discarded.
But you remain the same,
and your years will never end."
PSALM 102:25–27

TABLE OF CONTENTS

ACKNOWLEDGMENTS

This book, in so many ways, represents the input of a variety of mentors. Perhaps one of the most profound influences on my life is a man by the name of Campbell McAlpine, whom I regard as one of the clearest prophetic voices of the latter half of the twentieth century. For me, as well as many of my comrades, this man has stood out as an uncompromising voice to a church that has often lost its singular vision of Jesus.

Others, too, have played significant roles in my life, whetting in me an appetite for God and awakening in me an understanding of how he works. I think of Albie Pearson, who tutored me in my early years of ministry; Joy Dawson, who showed me as a young buck that I could hear the voice of God and follow him whole-heartedly; Pastor Desmond Evans, a gifted Welsh Bible teacher, who believed in me when I didn't really believe in myself; Iverna Tompkins, another gifted Bible teacher, who, to me and many others, has been like a great aunt giving out incredible bits of wisdom at exactly the right moment; Rick Howard, who instilled in me a desire to communicate the Word of God; and David Reece-Thomas, who was there many times as a safe haven when I couldn't see my way.

But perhaps my greatest friend and mentor has been my own father, Gerry Fry, who showed me by example that humility is the grace that unlocks all other graces and taught me what it was like to hunger for God's presence more than anything else. A son couldn't have asked for a better dad. To these and so many more, I express deep appreciation.

I also want to thank all of my Messenger Fellowship colleagues who have collaborated with me on many ventures around the globe; they have been an enriching source of friendship and support.

Over the years, many secretaries and associates have labored diligently on a wide variety of manuscripts that were never published; but they all said that maybe one day some of my random musings might just find their way into print. Lila Hedlund, Helen Lallo, Jeannie Russell, my sisters, Shannon Hoye and Candace Strubbar, Terry Wardley, Beverly Kaemmerling, Shari Hicks, and most importantly, Libby Whittaker, who has served my wife and me untiringly for the past seven years—to all of you who wrote pages and pages of copy that never saw the light of day—here's to you!

I want to express a deep sense of gratitude to my friend and editor, David Hazard, who more than anyone else has instilled in me the love of writing. He has been a welcome source of encouragement as well as a discerning instructor who has guided me through the sometimes exhausting process of producing a manuscript, always bringing to my disjointed thoughts a modicum of clarity.

I also want to thank Don Jacobson, president of Multnomah Publishers, and the rest of the crew at Multnomah for so enthusiastically believing in this book and giving it a broader voice. I especially want to thank Tracy Sumner for championing this project within Multnomah and for painstakingly crafting it in its final stages.

Finally, I want to thank my wife, Nancy, who for twenty-three years now has been my biggest fan. She, too, has typed reams of copy for articles, books, and training manuals over the years. Far more than that, she has prayed me through numberless spiritual skirmishes, prodded me to believe God's promises in the face of countless challenges, and stood by me the many times I have felt utterly alone. Her affections have often been the sweetest expressions of our Father's love to me this side of paradise.

Thanks, too, to my three kids, Cameron, Kelsey, and Caleigh, who have sacrificed time with their dad, but who have been as enthused as I in getting a book out that would help others discover God's love.

I can say with Paul, "Thanks be to God, who always leads us in triumphal procession in Christ and through us spreads everywhere the fragrance of the knowledge of him" (2 Corinthians 2:14). My life has been guided by this one overarching thought: As people see what God is like, they cannot help but fall in love with him. Nothing else satisfies me like communing with God, receiving by his grace glimpses of his nature, while spending time face-to-face with him. Mining the Scriptures for every gem of insight into his character is the kind of pursuit that is an ever expanding journey of joy—the more one knows, the more one wants to know. Everything flows from *him*, so it is with great ease and enthusiasm that I can say, "To God be the glory!"

FOREWORD

Nothing about this book—except *everything*—surprises me.

Those are carefully and sincerely chosen words, and not merely a cleverly constructed "hook" to catch your attention. Allow me for a moment to explain, and then "loose you" to stroll *through* (for refreshing) or to search *into* (for depth) this uncommonly enriching book.

Nothing in this book surprises me because...

It was about twenty years ago when I first met Steve Fry. There sat this teenage boy, seated at the piano as he began to lead a rather large gathering of pastors and spiritual leaders into the opening segment of the evening worship. To be honest, I was a little disappointed. At least, at first.

Now hear me, please. I'm neither snobbish nor condescending toward teenagers—indeed, to this day I'm still amazed and humbled to be invited to speak to large groups of them. But it did seem to me that the many hundreds of churchmen and churchwomen assembled should have recommended that the event planners engage a more seasoned leader for so significant a part of the gathering. So, I was dubious at the beginning. And it wasn't because of the young leader's skills (which were immediately obvious and remarkable), but because his young age seemed to predict a deficiency of adequate substance (spiritual clout, maturity, or weightiness) to warrant his leading such a group of spiritually experienced worshipers and warriors.

It was between the second and third song led by the teenager (whose name I later discovered was Steve Fry) that I found myself in a rather gratifyingly stunned state. *This kid really is something,* I thought. *There's a meatiness to his remarks, a tangible* something (*better,* Someone) *verifiably present in his demeanor, and a studied quality of genuine passion for God in his music.* Entering in with more relaxed confidence in his leadership, I not only experienced God's goodness and presence along with the others present, but I was marked with a deep impression: This young man's *love* for God is born of a David-like passion to *know* God.

Suffice it to say, my disappointment was not only dissolved, but that night I felt I had found a full partner, a full generation younger than I, in that passionate pursuit of God that presses beyond form and fashion and cries out to know the one who awaits us in the inner place behind the veil. That "boy" taught us one of his own compositions that night (without mentioning it was his or making a self-serving reference to God having "given me this song"). That lyric says all of the above better than any words of my own:

Abba, Father! Abba, Father!
Deep within my heart I cry.
Abba, Father! Abba, Father!
I will never cease to love You!

The countenance of that youthful leader and the abiding content of his character and songs that I came to discover in Steve have made it impossible for me to ever again be surprised by the richness of his ministry. So it is that I have begun to peruse this enormous small book with a sense of renewed awe—awe over the Holy Spirit's ability to make mere human words produce heart-searchings, soul-awakenings, and mind-stretchings all through a fresh look at the wonders of our almighty and all-loving Father God.

Thus, *everything* in this book surprises me because…

Steve continues to do here what I "caught" him doing that night long ago, but what he has been doing with integrity through his faithful ministry for over two decades. Whether ministering the Word of God, composing to lead us in the worship of God, or—as here—writing to invite us deeper into the wonder of God, his extraordinary gift for drawing us to hunger more for God brings us to blessing.

In reading these pages, I have been stirred to yet another dimension of hunger for God and a desire to seek him yet more deeply. And, of course, it is always exactly this order of pursuit that results in any of us coming to glimpse more of God himself—where *everything* is a new surprise! But this is no casual matter, and these pages are not casually written. They awake a hunger because they have been born of it. And hunger is the key. Not information. Not curiosity. Not short-termed dallyings into the supernatural.

To read this book is to discover a summons to such hunger— that which stirs a deeper, more passionate quest for God. And it is thereby we find ourselves being led to *his* place of eventual, certain satisfaction. Jesus said so: In calling us to acknowledge our own emptiness apart from God, our Savior guaranteed the reward for all who come in such honesty, saying, "Blessed are those who hunger and thirst for righteousness, for they shall be filled" (Matthew 5:6, NKJV).

It is there we find certainty and wholeness, there that peace and healing begin to overspill the soul, and there that we begin to drink at the only true fountain of joy. To be drawn to hunger to know God more fully—and to pursue that attraction—is to be drawn to discovery, to find a new unveiling of his loving purpose for each of us, and to find a new unfolding of his life and power in us.

So, receive this book's invitation: Open up—yourself as well as these pages. Come and see more of the wonder of God—and find your hunger for him increasing. He's the God of everything you or I can ever yearn for—from being a healer of our hearts to becoming a Friend we can know face-to-face.

JACK W. HAYFORD
THE CHURCH ON THE WAY
THE KING'S SEMINARY
VAN NUYS, CALIFORNIA

INTRODUCTION

My wife, Nancy, and I have three delightful children. Like most parents, some of our dearest memories are those times when we were anticipating their arrival: buying baby clothes, painting the nursery, and…attending birthing classes together.

We were on pins and needles the first time we attended the birthing class. *What was labor really going to be like?* we wondered. Nancy was well into her first pregnancy the day she and I first traipsed into the hospital room where we were instructed on how to deliver this child with a minimum amount of pain. Over the course of several weeks, we learned how to breathe during labor and how to "ride" contractions. We were even told when *not* to show up at the hospital.

The first few sessions were fun. But one night the instructor began to talk to us about "transition," that point in labor when the woman dilates seven to ten centimeters, bringing her right to the point of delivery. As all mothers know, this is the most painful time of labor. Our instructor told us that at this critical moment, it was imperative that we establish a *focal point*. A focal point was necessary, she said, in order to manage the labor well.

"Pick a picture on the wall to focus on, or a flower in the vase—anything to help you get your mind off the contractions," she told us. As I recall, the instructor was quite serious about all this.

The moment came when our son Cameron announced his immediate readiness to enter this world. Hours later, transition hit Nancy like a freight train. *Focal point,* I said to myself. *We've got to have a focal point!* I had been coaching Nancy throughout her labor, but now the whole ordeal shifted up in intensity. As I frantically searched for an appropriate focal point that would see her through her pain, she grabbed my arm and whispered, "You know, honey, I think I just want to look at your face while I'm going through this. I want your face to be my focal point."

Throughout our lives we will experience the joy of "birthing" many things—starting families, launching careers, founding ministries. We will also endure seasons of pain. Not every question will be answered; not every wound assuaged. But there is a focal point that will see us through. It is the wonder of God himself!

Understanding and delighting in God is the headwater of life. Everything flows from a relationship with God. Today, there is a great deal of attention being given to prayer, reaching the unreached, and the church's desperate need for revival. But it is only a passionate relationship with God that will fuel our prayer campaigns when we bear little fruit; only a passionate relationship with God that can protect our worship from becoming mere emotional release; only a passionate relationship with God that will guard us from executing lifeless strategies; only a passionate relationship with God that will lace our ministry with joy for a lifetime.

Richard Rolle, the great fourteenth-century mystic, put it this way: "God is of infinite greatness, more than we can think...whenever the heart begins to burn with the desire for God, she is made able to receive the uncreated light and, inspired and fulfilled by the gifts of the Holy Spirit, she tastes the joys of Heaven."

God is birthing new things in and through his church, and many of us are feeling the contractions: We feel it in the rapid, moral deterioration of our society; we feel it in the accelerated velocity of technological change; we feel it in a certain loss of intimacy and community with those around us. Some feel like the swirl of events is snatching them from their comfort zones; others feel pinched between the safe and predictable images of yesteryear and the unavoidable certainty of constant flux in a chaotic future. In the midst of it all, God is doing new things: giving us creative ways to impact our world, new angles from which to explore timeless truths, and fresh vigor to pursue unity with one another. But the only constant that will nourish our desire to walk faithfully in all of this is an intense focus on God.

I've had the privilege of being involved in theatrical productions from time to time. During one of these productions, a ballerina told me that when a ballet dancer pirouettes, she must have a focal point; she must fasten her gaze on something while she turns her body, lest she spin out of control. I have often watched the graceful movements of a ballet company performing *Swan Lake* or the *Nutcracker*. There is just something special when a prima ballerina flawlessly pirouettes, spinning with such form and balance. What is her secret? The focal point. Fixing her eyes on someone in the audience or a prop on the stage, she twirls with abandon, turning her head only at the last moment of each graceful spin in order to maintain her poise.

Unless we focus on God, our lives, our families, the broad national coalitions we attempt to create, and the international mission initiatives we so eagerly pursue will ultimately spin out of control. It is only as we gaze intensely upon the wonder of who God is that we will be able to walk with a sense of balance and poise in a crazy world.

Centuries ago, an unknown writer wrote what has become a classic in Christian literature, *The Cloud of Unknowing*. His language to the modern ear sounds a bit strange, so I'll paraphrase: "Lift up your heart unto God," he said, "with a meek stirring of love; and seek Him for Himself, not for the Good He would give you. And look you! Be loathful to think on anything but God Himself, so that you will not trust in your own wits nor in the strength of your own will; but will work only out of pleasure you take in God himself."

Long ago, a man saw a burning bush from afar. As he gingerly stepped toward that bush, he heard a voice—the voice of the matchless Creator of the universe. As Moses gazed on that sight, the brilliant glow of the divine glory caught him in its beam. The I AM was present! It was glory so comforting he could divulge his deepest misgivings, yet so compelling he knew nothing would ever satisfy him again. As another faithful saint, Thomas à Kempis was to exclaim hundreds of years later, "Vanity of vanities, all is vanity, except to love God, and him only to serve."

As you reflect on the beauty and majesty of God through these pages, may you find him to be as comforting and compelling as have millions throughout the ages. For once you see him as he is, you cannot help but fall in love with him.

Chapter 1

⚭

THE WONDERS
OF GOD

"Holy, holy, holy is the Lord God Almighty,
who was, and is, and is to come."
REVELATION 4:8

*S*ome years ago, a pastor in whose church I was to speak met me at the local airport. As we pulled away from the terminal, he began talking a mile a minute, waving his hands and tapping my arm. Clearly he was excited about something. His sense of enthusiasm was contagious. What had captivated him were some recent spiritual discoveries. It was refreshing to listen to someone who was excited—not about his plans, or his church programs, but by what he'd learned about God.

"Over the past year, I have been transformed," he said. "I never knew God could be so fascinating. Yet it seems the more I discover about him, the more I realize I *don't* know. Have you ever felt that way, Steve?"

I assured him I had.

"For months and months now, I've just been riveted to this whole pursuit of knowing God. The funny thing is that as I have shared some of my most exciting discoveries with my colleagues, their responses have been so casual, almost flippant. I would tell them things I was finding out about God, and they would say, 'Oh, we learned that in seminary.' Here I am pressing into God for all I'm worth—and they seem so indifferent."

Sadly, such tepid responses are all too common, I thought.

"Well, I went to God the other day," he went on, "and said, 'God, here I am pressing right into your heart, and I hardly feel that I know you at all. And these other guys seem to have you all figured out, but they're so complacent about it.' Then this thought popped into my head— I believe it was God—*Anyone can think they see all of me—from a distance.*"

His statement hit me like the jolt of a stun gun. How true it was! Sometimes our spiritual placidity is mere smugness. We coast along, and over time we lose that sense of wonder that would surely grip us if we spent time looking into the depths of God, especially at his love toward us and his healing touch for those whom life has harmed.

For many of us, getting to know God sounds like tedious business—the domain of dour theologians pouring over dusty manuscripts. For others of us, time seems to slip so quickly through our fingers that we never quite get around to spending it with God, reading his Word, and reflecting on his goodness. This sounds rather boring to a lot of people. Quiet time with God often runs a distant second to an exciting movie on TV. Then again, many of us want quality time with God, but are uneasy with the solitude, for there we face our unanswered questions, our unresolved hurts, our unbridled drivenness, and, yes, our unconfessed sin. To us God is not the source of delightful fascination, but the reminder of our faults.

The book of Revelation is a keyhole through which we can peek at the wonders to come. Angelic hosts surround heaven's regal throne, exclaiming the majesty of God:

- sounds never heard by human ear reverberating through eternity,
- peel after peel of praise thundering God's majesty;
- the hushed whispers of reverent awe;
- the crescendo of song,
- each melody building on the last;
- chords colliding in ecstatic harmonies,
- intensifying with each modulation,
- moving from the serene to the sublime;
- every note resonating the wonder of God!

These creatures are permanently caught in a transfiguration, utterly mesmerized by the one they worship. For time beyond time, they have been worshiping God with no apparent concern for their own existence, enraptured in the pull of divine fascination. That these beings never seem to think of themselves, but are singularly focused in their adoration of God, says something about God.

What kind of a God do we serve who can so totally empty these angels of all self-interest and hold them in rapt attention? He must be so incredibly absorbing, so uniquely satisfying that they give no thought to themselves, but are content to ceaselessly praise him.

How embarrassing, by comparison, is my self-centeredness.

As I reflected on my own worship experiences, I doubted that I could have repeated "Holy, Holy, Holy" for more than an hour. I would consider myself extremely spiritual if I could keep it up for two hours. Yet these creatures have never *ceased* to praise him—for millennia beyond counting! *How can they possess that capacity?* I wondered.

Reflecting on this Scripture makes me wonder if each time these creatures cry "Holy," God is moved to reveal a facet of his character they have never seen. For as the apostle Paul reminds us in Ephesians 3:10, God's wisdom is manifold. And every revelation of God makes them shout "Holy" all the more—which moves God to reveal even *more* of himself. And this has been going on for millennia—this amazing interplay of worship and revelation.

Imagine exploring the wonders of undersea mountains, volcanic fissures, and coral reefs of the Pacific. Or the autumnal colors of a New England wood. Or the vast Serengeti in Africa. Or the immensity of China's Great Wall. God is wonderful beyond all this.

God is inexhaustible in his wonder!

There is a restlessness in all of us that prods us to seek God. We try to sedate that restlessness with a myriad of pleasures; we try to silence that restlessness through hours of labor; we try to ignore that restlessness and pretend that we are in fact quite at home in this material world. C. S. Lewis once asked this question:

Do fish complain at the sea for being wet? If they did, would the fact not strongly suggest that they had not always been, or would not always be, purely aquatic creatures? If you are really a product of the material universe, how is it that you don't feel at home here?[1]

The sea creatures don't complain, for they are in their element. The fact that we complain—the fact that we're restless—betrays just how ill at ease we are in a material universe apart from a relationship with the God who made it.

If you have lost your desire to worship God, perhaps you need to meet him in new facets of his personality and nature. Have you lost peace, happiness, and meaning? Allowing the wonder of God to flood your soul can restore to you the essence of life itself and give you strength for your spiritual journey.

Having eternal life means more than living forever: Jesus said eternal life is *knowing God*. It is what G. K. Chesterton called life's practical romance—the view of things that combines "an idea of wonder and an idea of welcome." That's the *romance* we can know of God—awed by his wonder and secure in his welcome! That is why again and again, the apostle Paul prayed that the churches would be blessed with the Spirit of revelation, wisdom, and understanding (Ephesians 1:17, 18).

Angela of Foligna, a disciple of St. Francis of Assisi, once said, "The first step to be taken by the soul who desires to draw near to God, is to learn to know God in very truth, and not only outwardly as though by the color of the writing. *For as we know, so do we love;* therefore if we know but little and darkly, if we reflect and meditate on Him only superficially and pleadingly, we shall in consequence love Him but little."

Lord, my heart does not always sing out in praise, for it is often choked with disappointment. My heart is not always tender to your overtures of love because it is often hardened by angers big and small. My heart is not always turned toward you, for I fear that to really embrace you is to see not your glory, but my destitution. Oh, God, restore to me the joy of knowing you. I open my heart to you now. Create in me a hunger for you like I've never known, so that my heart can sing, can listen, and can embrace you once again.

QUESTIONS TO PONDER:

1. Have you ever thought of God as fascinating?

2. Have you found your wonder at the person of God waning? Why or why not?

3. What factors could distract you in your pursuit of God?

4. What steps could you take to reignite your love for and wonder of God?

Chapter 2

HE GIVES ETERNAL LIFE

*"Now this is eternal life: that they may know you,
the only true God, and Jesus Christ, whom you have sent."*
JOHN 17:3

*I*n the Hollywood musical *Scrooge*, the Ghost of Christmas Present invites the old miser to a sumptuous Christmas feast. As Scrooge imbibes and gorges himself, the ghost, appearing as a jovial Father Christmas, sings a rousing song:

> I like life; Life likes me;
> Life and I fairly fully agree.

For a brief moment, Scrooge is transformed from the humbug curmudgeon to a rollicking merrymaker, caught up in the celebration of life as it was meant to be lived.

Life. The thrill of skiing down a freshly powdered slope. The sweetness of a summer snooze in a hammock. The laughter of friends. The satisfaction of a job well done. Life:

- where reality lives up to our expectations;
- where we find a satisfying rhythm between what we are and what we do;
- where we find a sense of fulfillment and genuine happiness;
- where integrity is enjoyable and relationships are satisfying.

We all want a good life. But John took note of the way Jesus defined real living—and what our Lord promises is something more than we can imagine. The most satisfying images we could conjure up don't begin to compare with what God has given us, and that is eternal life. That's far more than simply living forever—it's living a *fulfilled* forever. The emphasis here is not just eternity, but *life*—a life that begins the moment you and I meet Jesus.

Life is all that death is not. Death suggests isolation and loneliness, something that is cold and unfeeling, cut off from all that is energetic and vibrant, where anxiety robs us of peace, and anger robs us of joy. Life is goodness in abundance.

At least that was what God intended.

Sadly, many people live large parts of their lives in a state of death—lonely, feeling rejected and uncared for, suspicious of intimacy, even hardened in their hearts. Death in this context is not the cessation of biological functions; it is the loss of joy and innocence. When we place our trust in a close friend, and that person betrays us, something in us dies. Or when it becomes apparent that we will never realize the dream to which we aspired, again, something in us dies. Death is the promotion never received, the confidence betrayed, the callousness of a son or daughter, or the agony of a missed opportunity that causes us to die a hundred times inside.

If offered a chance to escape from the misery of a meaningless existence, most of us would jump at it and ask, "What can I do? How much can I pay? Where can I sign on the dotted line? How can I really live?" The answer is not found in a sense of liberated personhood, in human friendship, in personal accomplishment, in retreating to some exotic vacation spot, or in receiving a lavish inheritance.

When asked the question "Do you really want to live?" we race to the counter with all our hidden desires of wealth, pleasure, and prestige—only to hear Jesus' response: "This is life—*that you know God.*" When we hear this, we stop dead in our tracks. Somehow God and life don't seem to belong together; they're not part of the same song. "God" suggests everything that is wrong with me; even worse, "God" sometimes suggests why I'm so miserable.

We want life, but sometimes we are not willing to make the journey that will get us to real life. The truth is that many of us don't really want to get that close to God. For some, it is because they are afraid of him. They remember all their broken promises to him to do better and the times they failed over and over again. Or perhaps they recall images of a vindictive God scoping the earth for someone to judge, and that stirs uneasy feelings of shame lurking in the shadows of their souls. Uncertain about where they stand with God, they keep a healthy distance between themselves and him. To suggest that knowing God is synonymous with satisfying living is beyond their comprehension. *How can one who evokes such feelings of dread be the source of my fulfillment?* they wonder. To them God may be a Father, but he is a stern one who must always be appeased.

For others, the problem isn't fear, but anger—some unanswered prayer, unresolved hurt, or the loss of someone they held dear. They hold God responsible for these things and become resentful, even bitter—bitter at the injustice they have suffered, bitter at the opportunities they feel they've never had, bitter at the seemingly unrelenting hardships they go through without receiving a satisfying answer from God. Again, to suggest that knowing God is life in its most fulfilled form only irritates them more. *How can a God who has allowed me to go through so much pain be the source of my happiness?* they fume.

There are still others who know enough of God to be secure in his Fatherhood and in the knowledge that they have eternal life, but who simply have grown weary with life here and now. Those who have labored for fruit still unseen; those who have persevered without reward; those who are subject to the harassment of the enemy and the rejection of people; those who have learned the art of enduring, but have not known the thrill of overcoming—to them the idea that knowing God is the key to a deeply satisfying life *now* sounds good, but it is no longer believable. They endeavor to *serve* him, but have lost their ability to *enjoy* him. *How can I return to the place where the joy of the Lord is my strength?* they ask.

It is these people—the fearful, the angry, the weary—to whom I want to speak: to those riddled with disappointment; to those who love God, but have lost the passion for his purpose; and to those whose lives are simply out of focus.

It is not so much that Jesus Christ *gives* us the answers—he *is* the answer. We who believe that life will be wonderful if we can just solve our problems and eliminate our hassles may not realize that cultivating friendship with God is actually the way to have the kind of life we crave.

Only when we set aside our fears, resentments, and even fatigue and strive to *know* him and seek him simply for the wonder of who he is—not to get answers, or meet our needs, or receive strength—will we suddenly find our fears, anger, and weariness subsumed by the deluge of joy that comes from discovering God.

Nicholas of Cusa, a church leader who lived many centuries ago in a time very different from our own, spoke words that are as relevant today as they were in his time. Caught up in the exhilaration of God's love for him, he wrote, "Life eternal is none other than that blessed focus where You never cease to behold me, yes, in secret places of my soul. With You, to behold is to give life, to unceasingly impart the sweetest love of You, and inflame me to love You by love's imparting…."

Let's ask the Holy Spirit to give us some fresh glimpses of what God is like, remembering what the Lord said through a prophet centuries ago:

> "Let not the wise man boast of his wisdom or the strong man boast of his strength or the rich man boast of his riches, but let him who boasts boast about this: that he understands and knows Me…," declares the Lord. (Jeremiah 9:24)

How about you? Are you weary and disappointed with life? Then try to find appropriate Scriptures that reaffirm the goodness of God's character. We've all endured times when we've been frustrated with life and have blamed God. What steps can we take to keep our hearts tender to his voice? How can we maintain that calm assurance in the Father's grace that sees us through life's pressing challenges?

Lord, bring me to the place where I can truly enjoy you.
Grant me a heart that longs to know you, the kind of heart
that King David had when he pined for your presence in the
desert—"Your love is better than life" (Psalm 63:3).
I know I may rush about looking for all kinds of things
to satisfy my deepest yearnings, but I realize that
at the end of the day, all I really need is you.

QUESTIONS TO PONDER:

1. By and large, do you enjoy life? Why or why not?

2. Do you tend to see God more as a loving Father or a stern ruler? Why do you see him that way?

3. Where or to whom do you turn in times of disappointment and distress?

4. How can striving to know God help you deal with life's problems?

Chapter 3

THE BOUNDLESS GRACE OF GOD

Therefore, since we have been justified through faith,
we have peace with God through our Lord Jesus Christ,
through whom we have gained access by faith
into this grace in which we now stand.
ROMANS 5:1–2

*J*esus loves me this I know, for the Bible tells me so…"

The simple refrain of an innocent song beckons us to really *believe* God loves us.

But anyone who has walked on *terra firma* for very long has accumulated enough experiences to see innocence killed. Most of us file "Jesus Loves Me" in the church nursery department. As much as we might believe in God's love, we feel deeply insecure in our relationship with him. We remember our unforgivingness to the neighbor who wronged us and Jesus' statement, "Unless you forgive...." We hear the preacher say, "If you don't pray, you won't have any power in your life" and recall the many times in the previous week we could have prayed and didn't. Or someone treats us rudely and instead of responding with kindness, we spit right back at that person. And when we blow it, a calliope of accusing voices pipes in tones at once shrill and shaming:

"I knew I couldn't measure up!"

"I've pushed God too far!"

"Why even try?"

Here is the conflict.

Imagine yourself as a little child knowing you've disappointed your dad. You want to be enfolded in his arms, yet you back away from his affections. So are we with God. Over time, our attempts to please him and our failure to do so drain us of any zest we originally had for God. We become like yo-yos that have run out of spin at the end of fate's finger. Resignation has replaced hope in our hearts.

Why is God's love so hard to receive? Why is it that the more I *try* to please God, the less I *seem* to please him? The answer can be found in one simple word at which devils curse and angels stand in awe: *Grace*. It is grace that opens us up to the love of God. Without grace, we may believe in his love, but we will never allow it to revolutionize our lives.

Grace is the fact of God's favor even when we don't deserve it. Grace is the truth that God's favor is not something we earn, but something we already have. Yet, if there is one primary tactic the enemy uses to keep us off balance, it is deceiving us into doubting God's favor. We still feel his favor is something we must earn. We have a "He-loves-me; he-loves-me-not" view of God.

For years as a youth pastor, I unknowingly—and quite inno-cently, I might add—encouraged this somewhat distorted view of God. Many of us, youth leaders and teenagers alike, were not con-tent in a youth group of substantial size to be a prepubescent day-care center—we wanted to be as radical as the early Christians in the book of Acts. To that end, we emphasized God's *standards* in measurable disproportion to his *grace* and preached discipleship as the true test of conversion. It wasn't that it was wrong information; it was just dispensed in the wrong order. Living by God's standards became the *means of obtaining* God's favor rather than a response *to* God's favor. Most of us were radical, but insecure, and in time it caught up with us.

My insecurity caught up with me some years later, surprisingly, in the security of my own family room, with the most nonthreat-ening person I know: my wife, Nancy. We were engaged in a dis-cussion—the kind that married couples often have, when the decibel level reaches 110 and the thermometer registers numbers found only in Phoenix, Arizona, in July. As the argument intensi-fied, I made some unkind remark to her. Of course, she retorted in kind. Barbs flew like darts for the next few minutes until she retired to the kitchen to nurse her wounds.

Since I had to preach that night, I stomped into my study to finish my preparation. I began to pray, but I hadn't been on my knees ten minutes when I knew what I had to do. If I didn't apolo-gize to Nancy right then and there, I would never be able to preach with conviction that night. So I slunk into the kitchen where she was dutifully preparing my dinner, stared sheepishly at my feet, and told her I was sorry for what I had said.

My lips were forming the last syllable of the last word of my apology when she turned around, looked me straight in the eyes, and said, "I know why you're apologizing to me! You just want to make sure God blesses you tonight!" There is no word or assortment of words that can describe the shock that went through my system. She nailed me, and instantly years of theology went out the window. She wasn't saying that apologizing wasn't important—we all know it's essential. But in that one pointed statement she unmasked me: I was being obedient to a right truth for the wrong reasons. I was making restitution not as a response of love to God and my wife, but out of the fear of failing in that evening's ministry.

What would have happened had I not apologized to my wife? I suggest that the Lord would have greatly blessed my efforts that night; then afterward, he would have prodded me: "Didn't I bless you tonight? In the light of my grace toward you, could you not have been gracious toward your wife?"

I would have been wondrously devastated. I would have seen my sorry attitude in the light of his wonderful grace and would have quickly made things right with Nancy. I would have been amazed at a love that extended favor while at the same time convicting of sin.

That is God's way, you know. *He has chosen to conquer by love, not coerce through threats.*

Yet such affirmations of God's unconditional love strike a hollow chord in many skeptical hearts. In the minds of many who faithfully attend church and dutifully read their Bibles, God's favor is something they must earn through right living. They try so hard to do the right thing, but still feel so insecure. At times, we as spiritual leaders unthinkingly play off of this sense of insecurity in an attempt to rekindle in believers the flame of commitment.

For example, we've all heard well-meaning preachers exclaim that if we don't pray, we'll have no spiritual power in our lives. This is absolutely true. No one would disparage the link between a life of prayer and a ministry of power. But is it God's intention to induce us to pray by threatening us with a lack of power? If we pray only to achieve spiritual effectiveness—or out of fear of not achieving it—what kind of obedience is that? In such subtle ways, we leaders tend to manipulate behavioral change. On the surface the results are gratifying: Prayers are lifted, Bibles read, and principles obeyed. But the true motivation behind all the activity is simply to ensure a sense of rightness with God. In our zeal we have unwittingly encouraged another round of legalism, the rewards of which we are now reaping in the spiritual disinterest of our children.

This whole mindset exposes an undercurrent of insecurity, of never being quite sure where we stand with God.

It's not enough to obey right principles; we need to obey for the right reasons. For the Father doesn't want us to obey out of fear, but out of love.

I am awed by the wonder of your grace! To think that you have rescued me once and for all from the treadmill of personal performance. To know that I no longer have to earn your favor, but that you have lavished your favor on me, leaves me speechless with gratitude. When I see how vast your love is in the ways grace works, it not only humbles me, but infuses me with a passion to lean on you for everything and in that place of dependence on you, to strive to never hurt through my waywardness a God who loves me so deeply.

QUESTIONS TO PONDER:

1. What does it mean to you to realize that Jesus loves you *unconditionally?*

2. How do you respond to God when you know you've messed up? Do you run *to* him or *away* from him?

3. Do you respond more positively to threats or to loving correction? Why?

4. What does the word *grace* mean to you?

Chapter 4

HE'S THE
HEARTMENDER

But now in Christ Jesus you who once
were far away have been brought near....
EPHESIANS 2:13

*R*ejection is one of life's deepest heartbreaks. To love someone only to have that love spurned cuts deep into the most innocent part of our heart. To do our best only to be ignored shocks us to our core. To want to belong to a group only to be excluded evokes a throbbing ache inside.

I am not wanted! As that monotonous cadence resounds within us in a dozen different ways, we slowly cordon ourselves off from others, revealing ourselves very selectively in order to minimize the risk of rejection. We assume various roles, trying to be somebody other than who we are in order to find a persona that's acceptable to others.

We give that it might be given back to us.

We pout when we feel others withdrawing from us.

We learn the art of heaping guilt on those whose attention we crave.

Then the futility of such maneuvers catches up with us, and we lash out in anger at the injustice of it all, which only further isolates us from people and propels us to a new round of dishonesty, manipulation, and loneliness. Jaded, we find ourselves echoing comedienne Lily Tomlin: "We're all in this alone."

This is all a million light years from God's original intention. God created a garden where his children, knowing the security of his loving embrace, would freely give love even as they had received it. Yet the joy God intended for us vanished when our first parents succumbed to the deception of the tempter.

When we read the account of Adam and Eve's fall, it is all too easy to view it one-dimensionally: They disobeyed and suffered the consequences. In truth, it was far subtler than that. For when Satan tempted Eve, he not only tempted her to rebel, he also provoked in her a sense of anticipated rejection. He goaded Eve to question God's love. "Has God said…?" he asked her. If we could peek into her mind, perhaps we would hear her struggle: *Why is God withholding the fruit of one tree? Is there something he isn't telling me? Can't he trust me? Am I not worthy of the Lord's confidence?*

The enemy's tactic was not only to entice Eve to disobey, but to agitate her to distrust. And this windstorm of questions stirred up that sense of rejection. The tragedy was that Eve, believing the lie and imagining God's rejection, fell prey to the enemy's trick.

The *anticipated* sense of rejection became the sense of *deserved* rejection. Adam followed her in the disobedience, and they found themselves hiding, pathetically trying to cover themselves with fig leaves. Suddenly they came face-to-face with a new master: fear. And man has been running and hiding and trying to cover himself ever since.

Because of this sense of deserved rejection, fear has ravaged society like an acute infection, producing a race feverishly driven by one overriding purpose: self-preservation. It has driven some to prejudice and bias as a means of self-protection; it has provoked others to jealousy and competition, using others' failures to their own advantage.

This contagion of fear has poisoned the healthy relationships God intended men to have. Relationships have been established not on the basis of love, but as a means to determine one's self-worth. People have been used to bolster sagging egos, and then discarded when the risk of hurt became too great. Rejection has become a pox on the human race and is just as basic to the misery of the human condition as rebellion.

Rebellion calls for repentance; rejection calls for healing. How was God to provide this healing? What was the remedy to this infection of rejection? Again, the answer is found in the wonder of God's grace; he found a way to heal the rejection by offering its opposite—acceptance. *Unconditional acceptance!* The New Testament calls this *justification*. That word means a lot of things, but the bottom line is that once we've completely yielded ourselves to Christ Jesus, God accepts you and me with no strings attached.

G. Campbell Morgan was perhaps one of the greatest Bible

expositors of the first half of the twentieth century. Before he enjoyed the esteem of his colleagues and countrymen, he endured some early rounds of rejection as a young man. When he was invited to preach a sermon to prove he was worthy to enter the Methodist ministry, he was scheduled to speak in an auditorium that seated more than one thousand people. Only seventy-five showed up, and his performance was pathetic. He failed miserably and was rejected from the ministry. Despondent at his failure, he wired his father, "Rejected!" His father quickly wired back: "Rejected on earth—accepted in heaven."

Accepted in heaven! The fact that we've been unconditionally accepted seems too good to be true. Deep inside, we feel most unacceptable. To speak of a grace that brings us to the Father's heart, where we are enveloped in his loving arms, seems closer to a Cinderella story than it does to biblical truth. But grace is not a fairy tale. In fact, God's grace revealed to us is not just an expression of his love, but of his wisdom. He wasn't simply being kind in making a way for us to know his unconditional acceptance. He was being just plain smart. For God knew that unconditional acceptance was the only thing that would heal us of rejection's infection.

Lord, I pause for a moment in your presence. Bring to mind any area in my life where I am responding to others out of a sense of rejection. Help me recall any episodes, past or present, that the enemy may be using to provoke withdrawal, insecurity, or even arrogance in me—responses that I so often employ to salve the wounds of rejection in my own way.

I know that ultimately I will he healed, as by faith I embrace your grace and there find that I am accepted unconditionally by the Creator of the universe. So now, one by one, I give you each feeling of rejection. Bathe me thoroughly in your grace!

QUESTIONS TO PONDER:

1. Can you remember how you felt during a time of rejection or heartbreak? How have those memories affected you?

2. How has the fear of rejection affected your relationships—with other people and with God?

3. Are you secure in the fact that God will never reject you?

4. Do you, because of God's love, see yourself as *acceptable*? Why or why not?

Chapter 5

FREE TO CHANGE

Where the Spirit of the Lord is,
there is freedom.
2 CORINTHIANS 3:17

The story is told of an eight-year-old boy who was just about as naughty as they come. This kid was evil, mean, rotten, and nasty! So much so that as Christmas Day approached, his mother informed him that Santa was not going to leave him any presents under the tree. Well, this irked Junior, so he ran upstairs to his bedroom, pulled a sheet of paper out from his little desk, and proceeded to write Jesus a letter to ask him to persuade Santa to give him presents for Christmas. His first draft went something like this:

Dear Jesus,

    I promise to be a good boy for one year if you tell Santa Claus to give me presents for Christmas.

He looked at that letter and knew good and well he wasn't going to last for a year. So he pulled out another sheet of paper and tried again:

Dear Jesus,

    I promise to be a good boy for three months....

He looked at this letter a little harder, but still knew that there was no way he was going to be a good boy for three months. Draft after draft, the little imp wrote, each successive draft promising goodness for increasingly shorter spans of time. Finally, in exasperation, he pulled out one more sheet of paper and wrote:

Dear Jesus,

    I promise to be a good boy for one whole day if you tell Santa to give me presents for Christmas.

He thought he could probably make it for one day. But bounding out of his bedroom, he paused at the top of the stairs, realizing that he wouldn't make it for even one day. So what does an evil, mean, rotten, nasty kid do when confronted with such a dilemma? Well, he ran down the stairs, took the little figurine of the Virgin Mary from the nativity set on the mantel, ran back to his bedroom, pulled one last sheet of paper from his drawer, and wrote:

Dear Jesus,

    If you ever want to see your mother again....

Most of us would never resort to such obvious manipulation to get God to do what we want. Deep down, we know that we deserve punishment, and this sense of deserved retribution evokes strong fears and insecurities. We know that God is infinitely good and that we are hopelessly self-centered. We know that without the Cross of Jesus, banishment from the garden of his heart is all we could ever expect. Yet, by his grace through Christ's death on the cross, we've been brought near.

One would think that because the Son of God died such a cruel death for us, we would feel fairly secure in our relationship with him. But it's often our sense of deserved punishment that leaves us riddled with insecurities. And if we do have a tender heart toward God, our dilemma is all the more poignant as we desperately try to assuage that realization by trying harder to be righteous. The irony is that the more we try to be righteous, the less power we seem to have to be so. That seems contradictory to us. Surely the more we focus on right living and adhering to biblical commands, the greater should be our conformity to those commands. Ah, but there is a subtle diversion whereby in shifting our focus to his commands, we actually lose sight of him—the only one with the *power* to enable us to obey in the first place.

Years ago I heard a wise old preacher say, "Love is giving someone else the power to change." Only when we have been freed from the need to perform will we be truly motivated to change. Oh, we may temporarily modify our behavior when we're trying to earn someone's favor or feel threatened by that person's displeasure. But eventually we'll react negatively to these pressures and either engage in wholesale rebellion or so completely conform to others' expectations that we cease to be genuine. It's all a matter of the heart. We are enveloped in God's embrace because of grace—and it is in that embrace that God's laws become no longer a code of conduct, but a desire of the heart.

God is in the business of turning our *have-to's* into *want-to's;* of creating a state of the heart in which we so revel in the wonder that God has accepted us that we find ourselves desiring his standards.

The apostle Paul reiterated this truth when he stated, "Where the Spirit of the Lord is, there is freedom" (2 Corinthians 3:17). The freedom he refers to is not the liberty to do what we want when we want; rather, it is the freedom to change. God's unconditional acceptance is not a sanctioning of our disobedience, but rather the starting point of lasting change.

God knows that we can only change in the context of freedom. That is why he has lavished his favor on us: so that we could be cut free from every insecurity, healed of rejection's residue, and released from every sense of abandonment that would keep us from truly changing.

Paul discussed this phenomenon and put a label on it: He called it the law of sin and death (Romans 8:1–2). Simply put, the more you try to live by the law, the more you ultimately *won't* live by the law. Under the Mosaic Covenant, the greater the attempt to live by the law, the more impossible it was to do so. But why? This seems to go against common sense. The problem for the Israelites was that the law became their primary focus instead of God himself. It's like trying to rid your mind of anxiety. The more you work at settling the anxiety, the more anxious you become. Why?

Because you are focusing on anxiety in the first place! *What you resist persists.*

Which brings us to an interesting point. Before Adam and Eve rebelled, they walked in unhindered communion with God. It was not his intention that humans become like him through a process of choosing good over evil. God did not want people at that time to even possess the knowledge of good and evil. Why? Because by knowing good and evil, they would center their focus on the need to be good and would inadvertently fall into self-centeredness. No, God designed people to become holy through single-minded fellowship with himself. Human character would be conformed to the center of human attention—God!

Self-righteousness is a great deal subtler and seems nobler than a holier-than-thou attitude. It can begin as a sincere preoccupation with one's personal conduct—with whether we're acting on right principles, constantly searching our hearts for sin, and so on. When taken to an extreme, such self-examination can become idolatrous. It is the idolatry of inner righteousness that breeds Pharisees. This may sound like a grand dilution of God's holy standards. But we're not dealing with the necessity of abiding by those standards—that's a given. It is *how* those standards are met and *why*. The attempt at righteousness on our terms serves only to reinforce rejection, which motivates us to try harder, which slowly paralyzes us in the coils of condemnation.

Grace is knowing that we have God's favor even when we don't deserve it; it is his unconditional acceptance of us. This may be difficult for us to comprehend because it seems to border on compromise. *"After all,"* we reason, *"if God has unconditionally accepted us, what does it matter if we obey or not? If God has already accepted us, then our conduct matters little."* Yet anyone who has ever come to such a conclusion has never even begun to see the profoundness of his grace.

Paul emphatically states that there is no condemnation for those in Christ Jesus (Romans 8:1). Freedom from condemnation does not come from strict adherence to the commands of God. Freedom comes from thirsting after the Spirit, who focuses us on Christ, which produces the overflow of obedience. As Oswald Chambers said, "God cannot deliver me while my interest is merely in my own character."[2] It is God alone who gives us the power to change, the desire to change, and the freedom to change. Or, as others more eloquent than I have stated it: We don't walk in the Spirit by overcoming the flesh; we overcome the flesh by walking in the Spirit.

Father, I confess that I often don't rest in your power to change me. So often I find myself trying to do the right thing and either getting frustrated with my inability to change or despondent, thinking I am a hopeless case. I want to be disciplined in my walk with you, but I know that discipline flows from my security in you; it's not the means of producing that security. Cleanse me of self-effort! Keep me on the edge of my need of your grace, and cultivate in me that deep dependence on your Holy Spirit, who makes me teachable.

QUESTIONS TO PONDER:

1. Do you ever find yourself striving to be "good"? What usually are the results of your efforts?

2. Do you often feel anxious over your seeming inability to make positive changes in yourself?

3. What is the relationship between holiness and fellowship with God?

4. What is it about God that motivates us to change?

Chapter 6

HE FREES US FROM GUILT

For if, by the trespass of the one man,
death reigned through that one man,
how much more will those who receive God's
abundant provision of grace and of the gift of
righteousness reign in life through
the one man, Jesus Christ.
ROMANS 5:17

I was fresh out of high school when the Watergate scandal broke. The revelations of subterfuge, which ultimately torpedoed Richard Nixon's presidency, shocked a generation. As the reality of the cover-up hit the nation square in the face, we soon became punch-drunk with an intensity of indignation unmatched in my lifetime. Though never formally charged, Richard Nixon remained an accused man in the public mind. President Ford later pardoned him, but Nixon was never able to shake the suspicions, the antagonism, and the repulsion of the millions who still considered him criminal.

Though pardoned, he was still subject to the court of human opinion, whose accusations he had to face for the rest of his life.

Tragically, many believers live out their lives just as Richard Nixon did—grateful for their pardon from God, but still vulnerable to Satan's accusations. We know we have been forgiven for breaking God's laws, but it's still hard to shake the enemy's guilt trips, and we desperately try to rid ourselves of that guilt much the same way we did as kids.

Do you remember how you responded to accusations as a little child? Maybe you recall a time your dad's stern voice summoned you, a four-year-old felon, to give an account of your waywardness. "I'll do better next time!" you'd pitifully blubber as you cried buckets of well-meaning tears. Or, perhaps you were like some of us who would set our little jaws, stiffen our little backs, and boldly declare, "I didn't do it!" We'd either promise to do better or justify our actions by defending or denying them.

Things haven't changed all that much as we've grown older. Most of the time we still respond to accusation in one of two ways: We either guarantee improved performance or we defend ourselves. Anything to alleviate that awful sense of guilt.

Satan knows this, of course, and that's why he seeks to accuse us at every turn. His very name, "the accuser," reveals what is perhaps his primary tactic against us as he strives to keep us off balance in our relationship with the Father. Always pointing a finger, he tries to wear us down until we are reduced to shadowboxing our discouragement.

But God in his grace addressed this tactic right from the get-go. For, you see, he didn't just pardon us—*he declared us righteous!* In other words, he declared us innocent right from the start. Had God simply pardoned us, we'd still be open to the enemy's accusations, and even though God would declare us not guilty every time, it would eventually become demoralizing going to trial over and over again. So God, in his big Father-heart of love, said, "I'm going to take care of the trial issue. I'm not going to just pardon you; I'm going to declare you *innocent,* so there will no longer be any grounds for accusation."

For years I struggled with this truth of Christ being my righteousness. Of course, I knew it was by grace that I was brought into relationship with Christ, but from then on, I felt it was up to me to become a righteous person. This was reflected in the way I prayed. In my mind I would see myself coming into the presence of God, but then realize I could not come into his holy presence until I had examined my heart for sin. So then I viewed myself as outside of his presence while I desperately attempted to deal with any sin in order to come into his presence. I continued to vacillate like this in my prayer times, until one day I discovered this startling truth: *I am declared righteous in Christ*—and declared so for very wise reasons.

Because God has declared me righteous, I no longer deal with sin in order to get into God's presence; now I am free to deal with sin because *I'm already in God's presence.* I am secure, resting on the Father's lap.

And there, of course, is where we truly find victory over sin. If I see the Father's face of love on the one hand, and, for example, my jealous attitude on the other, I will be on my way to lasting change, for I no longer want to hurt a God of love by being jealous.

No wonder so many people never conquer sinful attitudes. They're trying to deal with them in their own power and strength instead of from a position of absolute security in their relationship with God.

Back in my youth pastor days, I saw a cartoon in a Christian magazine that portrayed a hormonally supercharged adolescent ravenously devouring a pornographic magazine. God beamed down upon this young lad from the left-hand corner of the cartoon frame like a shaft of light. Between himself and the light of God bearing down on him, the teenager was holding up a cross. The caption read, "But I am righteous in Christ."

The cartoon was suggesting that the doctrine of being declared righteous invites us to compromise our lifestyles by behaving carelessly and that it really doesn't matter what we do because we are already declared righteous anyway. Many of us in our youth ministry agreed with the conclusion of this cartoonist, rebelling at a teaching we considered to be lukewarm garbage. Yet in our efforts to summon a generation to more committed discipleship, we abandoned what I later discovered is the cornerstone of security upon which good behavior is built.

Being declared righteous in Christ has nothing to do with sacrificing high moral standards in the name of cheap grace. It has everything to do with the wisdom of God, who has made it possible for us to be truly free and, in that context, to truly change.

By declaring us righteous, God removes all grounds for the enemy to harass and accuse us, while at the same time bringing us into his presence for good. From that place of security, we can find genuine victory over the sins that would destroy us. Far from opening a Pandora's box of compromise and spiritual license, this truth frees us to be conformed to the object of our affections, Christ himself, as we rest in the confidence that God, in the words of Pascal, will render us "incapable of any end other than Himself."

Guilt is such a paralyzing thing, O God.
It keeps so many bound, imprisoned by the consequences of
their choices. I don't minimize the consequences of my wrong
choices, nor shift the responsibility for my selfishness to others.
Yet in all of this, you have declared me righteous
precisely so that I will not be paralyzed by guilt.
So many in the world have misunderstood you,
thinking that you are a God who enjoys making them feel
guilty. In fact, you are the God of grace who has forever
resolved the guilt issue, if we but receive your gift of life
through Jesus. Far from ignoring my culpability, I realize only
too well how guilty I am. But grace upon grace, you have
declared me righteous! I won't try to understand it fully,
but I will take it by faith, knowing that the walk of
faith starts with believing what you have said about me:
that I am truly righteous in Jesus Christ!

QUESTIONS TO PONDER:

1. What do you believe is the proper place of the emotion of
    guilt in the believer's life?

2. Can you discern the differences between the enemy's accusa-
    tions and the Holy Spirit's conviction?

3. On what basis are we as children of God righteous?

4. How important is good, moral conduct in the life of the believer? What is that behavior an indication of in our lives?

Chapter 7

A GOD OF
FORGIVENESS

When we were God's enemies,
we were reconciled to him
through the death of his Son.
ROMANS 5:10

Recently, while hopscotching through the country, I found myself where I find myself too often these days—staring at the room service menu of some hotel. I decided to flip on the TV and turn to the local affiliate of a Christian television network. I was jarred by the image of an evangelist pacing back and forth across a platform, working up a sweat, hyping the audience with his fiery oratory. Intrigued, I sat down to listen to him tell the story of how he had recently been accosted by a journalist representing an influential newspaper.

Recognizing the evangelist at the airport, the journalist had requested an impromptu interview, which the evangelist magnanimously granted. The journalist asked him what he thought of a certain, well-known Christian leader. The evangelist told the crowd that the journalist was obviously baiting him, so he thrust his finger in the man's face like an UZI submachine gun and said heatedly, "You, sir, are the enemy!" The Christian audience present that night responded with boisterous applause, agreeing that this uncircumcised Philistine-of-a-journalist was indeed an enemy.

As they cheered their approval and the evangelist paced the length of the platform, obviously enjoying the sense of power such enthusiastic displays aroused, I couldn't help but ache inside. All I could hear being replayed in my mind was, *"You're the enemy!"* There was, to say the least, a noticeable absence of graciousness on the part of both speaker and listeners. It occurred to me that perhaps treating people as aliens is one of the biggest reasons we as the church have all but ceased to be heard by society.

The truth is that we Christians sometimes treat unbelievers as enemies—it's "them" against "us." This, of course, is a far cry from what the apostle Paul emphatically states in the fifth chapter of Romans, that, through Christ, all humankind has been reconciled to God, giving each of us the opportunity to receive God's gift of salvation. To put that another way, God's favor and forgiveness have been extended to all people everywhere because of what Jesus did on the cross. That is, indeed, good news.

We tend to think that forgiveness is purchased in the act of repentance—that before a person repents, he or she hasn't been offered the same forgiveness we as Christians enjoy. I suggest that this is a tragic distortion of the grace of God, and that it has had serious consequences in the church. Among other things, it has affected our evangelism. For if we approach people as those to whom God has not been reconciled through the Cross, we tend to treat them as hostile aliens rather than helpless slaves of the evil one. We develop an adversarial mindset, which further distances needy people from the Good News for which they long.

I can remember when this truth first impacted me. Sharing my faith was a chore because I treated unbelievers as part of the opposition. When I got hold of the fact that God's forgiveness had *already* been extended, I said to myself, *No wonder this is called the Good News.* A few days later, I found myself preaching on the streets of Mexico City, joyously declaring to a couple of hundred people gathered there in the plaza, "You are forgiven. Come and receive the free gift of God!"

Of course, this grace, which has provided so great a salvation, is not to be toyed with. Without a healthy fear of God, we can all too easily slip into the kind of flippancy so cynically expressed by the agnostic Voltaire when, speaking of God's forgiveness, he said, *"C'est son metier,"* which means, "It is his job."

A love so amazing that it has already provided forgiveness can be responded to only with genuine faith and repentance, the two appropriate responses to God's free gift. Furthermore, in the light of what God has done for us, it's little wonder that the writer of Hebrews dramatically described the awful consequences if we neglect "such a great salvation" (Hebrews 2:1–4). Still, for many of us as believers, the stress falls heavily on the fact that we have forgotten both the scope of his grace and the privilege of preaching the gospel. Our perception of grace has everything to do with whether we view evangelism as duty or joy.

If we treat unbelievers as enemies, they are going to respond as enemies. You may recall a particularly offensive movie entitled *The Last Temptation of Christ*, released several years ago. The portrayal of Christ's lustful fantasies about Mary Magdalene rankled many. It was Hollywood at its blasphemous best. At the time, thousands of Christians circled the wagons and shot back as vehemently as they could that secular society was the enemy and we were going to fight.

Maybe that's why movies like these are made in the first place; maybe this is why the church is scoffed at with such spite. It's not that I excuse such blasphemy, nor would I want to muffle the vigor of our protest. But I can't get rid of my uneasiness at the way we often relate to unbelievers—as enemies to be fought rather than captives to be delivered. Have we Christians lost a sense of graciousness because we ourselves have lost our sense of grace?

Let's remember that God has already been reconciled to every person we meet, and that they can freely receive his forgiveness—if they will. Our response to them may either help open the door of communication with God, or slam it shut even tighter.

Lord, help me be a bearer of good news! So stir my own soul
with the reality of your grace that I will be transformed.
Infuse me with an excitement to share my faith with others
like I've never had before, and help me to represent
you accurately to the unbelieving world.
So flow through me by your Holy Spirit that others
will be attracted to Jesus because of what they see in me.

QUESTIONS TO PONDER:

1. How do you view those who don't yet know Jesus Christ? Do you ever find yourself seeing them as some sort of enemy to be defeated?

2. How should we as Christians relate to those who don't know Christ?

3. On what basis have we been forgiven? When was that forgiveness made available to us?

4. What does it mean to you to be reconciled to God?

Chapter 8

A GIVING GOD

Will he not…graciously give us all things?
ROMANS 8:32

*D*on Evans, professor of philosophy at the University of Wales, told me this story many years ago.

A man had a dream, and in his dream he was taken to the portals of hell and ushered into a dank and depressing hotel lobby. While looking about at his dismal surroundings, he was intercepted by two ghoulish emissaries, who led him to a large banquet room. Upon entering this room, he was abruptly confronted with a kaleidoscope of chaotic impressions. The room was darkly lit, but he could tell that it extended far into the distance, and it echoed with the sounds of cursing and fighting. At the center of the room stood a long banquet table spread with the finest meal he could possibly imagine. All the delectable goodies he had ever seen or heard about covered the table, yet the pungent odor of decaying flesh kept him from enjoying the aroma of the feast set before him.

Through the misty candlelight he saw hundreds and hundreds of waiflike creatures, skeletal in their appearance, surrounding the table and trying to eat, but unable to do anything but swear and claw at each other. Upon closer examination, he saw that the utensils they were using extended about six inches beyond their arms. Every time they attempted to shovel spoonfuls of turkey dressing into their mouths, they couldn't manipulate the spoons beyond a certain point. At best, they could get the spoons to their shoulders before they ran out of arm span and clumsily dropped them on the floor. And there they just sat. Unable to eat any food, they were wasting away in an infinite agony of starvation.

Overwhelmed by this violent exhibition of futility, the man found himself suddenly transported to heaven. There he stood before an edifice so incredible, it defied description. He stood before heaven's hotel, which was grander than the Taj Mahal, more exquisite than a castle on the Rhine, more elegant than any palace he had ever seen or read about. As he walked into the lobby, a beauty that intensified with each second struck him. Two men in dazzling apparel met him and escorted him to a banquet hall. There he found a room gloriously lit, stretching far into the distance with a banquet table spread out before him. Content and at ease, hundreds of cherubic creatures, who seemed to be enjoying one another, surrounded this table. Upon closer inspection, he saw that they were using the same kind of utensils he had seen in hell and that each fork and spoon were about six inches longer than anyone's arm span. The difference, though, was that the creatures, instead of trying in vain to feed themselves, would take forkfuls of food and gently feed the creatures seated right across the table.

The moral of this story is obvious: As they gave, each one was nourished.

This is more than just an entertaining story: It describes the way God intended for this planet to work. When God's creatures consider others first, they find themselves truly cared for.

This story says a lot about what God is like. God is love. Not just *loving,* but *love.* Love is not a description of God—it is the essence of God. The practical demonstration of love is giving, and to say that God loves us is to say that he gives. The preservation of any created order, be it mankind or angels, is based on the priority of giving and considering oneself last. "Give and it shall be given unto you" is more than a good suggestion; it describes the eternal system.

It is profound to contemplate the fact that within the Godhead, the Father has never once thought of himself in terms of himself alone, but always in reference to the other two persons. This is all the more amazing to me when I consider just how self-centered I am.

If God has *always* considered himself last, what does that say about his motive for creating us? I suggest that when God made our first parents, he didn't make them because he needed more servants, or even more worshipers. He is not an egocentric God who is in constant need of greater adulation. I suggest that he didn't even make them because of his desire for companionship. He made them to *give* to them. No ulterior motives, no hidden agendas. He wanted to give himself unconditionally.

God has not changed. He has more to give than we'll ever have capacity to receive. And, amazingly, as we humbly receive, we are transformed into givers.

You and I cannot exhaust God's capacity and desire to give. We can impede it, but not exhaust it. You may be weary from the struggle or feel as if you've used up the currency of his forgiveness. You may feel as if you have pounded on heaven's door so long, desperately seeking to understand an unsolvable problem, that you have become an unwelcome pest. And you may feel as if you have come to the end of his storehouse of grace. Look again, and you will find a door that, when you open it, will reveal a landscape of love and kindness you've never imagined.

But remember, that door is marked "humility" and the handle, "dependence." For, in Saint Augustine's words, "God gives where He finds empty hands." Go to God as you are, with all your struggles and all your questions. Go, knowing God is just in all his ways. Go through that door and you will discover a God who, as the old hymn says, "giveth…and giveth…and giveth again."

Lord, so many who do not know you
think that you are a demanding, selfish God.
So many think you are but a cosmic boss on a power trip.
So many contest the idea that you are a God of love, feeling
that you made us all just so you would be adored all the more.
Help them and me to see that you are nothing of the kind!
But that in fact, you are a God who always thinks of himself

last. In the light of such incredible selfless love—
in the light of a God who gives beyond human
comprehension—how can I not give you
every fiber of myself in return?

QUESTIONS TO PONDER:

1. Do you think of God as a "giving" God? In what ways?

2. What are some things that God has given you personally? Physically? Emotionally? Spiritually?

3. Do you find yourself willing and able to go to God, expecting that he wants to give?

4. What hinders some from believing in a God who *wants* to give?

Chapter 9

GOD WAS
ONE OF US

The virgin will be with child
and will give birth to a son,
and will call him Immanuel.
ISAIAH 7:14

 hen Joan Osborne sang the Grammy-nominated song "One of Us" a few years back, it captured the desperate longing of a generation hoping against hope that there is a God and that he is somehow in touch with their ragged emotions.

What if God was one of us?
Just a slob like one of us?
Just a stranger on the bus,
Trying to make His way home....

Profane? Irreverent? Caustic disrespect? Or perhaps just the musings of a prodigal?

The God of the high-powered gospel pitch, the God of the quaint Christian coffee klatch, or the starch-shirted God repulsed by our appetites and indignant at our questions—that kind of a God evokes no interest in a generation that has turned coping into an art form.

Does God feel my pain?

Does he understand my anxieties?

Does he know why my head isn't screwed on straight?

Can he sense my fears when a friend offers me a joint?

Can he comprehend when I'm torn by temptations inside?

These are the questions countless people wrestle with, hoping there is a God out there personal enough to identify with their humanness, yet powerful enough to free them from themselves. They wonder, *Can a perfect God ever relate to such an imperfect me?*

He can—because he's already become like you! It's no longer a question of *What if God were one of us?* The fact is that *He's already become one of us!*

God came as a man and was rubbed raw by the incessant rejections of people; wearied beyond comprehension, carrying their stresses; numbed by the shocks of sickness and disease; and heartbroken beyond measure at the sheer ugliness of man's inhumanity.

It never loses its power to awe, this fact that God became man. To the skeptic, it never loses its stigma, either. But deep within, we all crave the assurance that God really understands what we're going through. That assurance could come no other way than by God becoming flesh.

Even Socrates, centuries before Christ's birth, concluded that if

God were to save us from ourselves, he would have to become a man and identify with human frailty. We call this the *Incarnation,* and, of course, far from reducing God to a human level, it enhances our sense of his majesty and our conviction that nothing is too hard for God, even becoming a man.

But what is even more amazing is that he became a *baby.* Now that is hard for secular man to swallow. The idea that God suddenly materialized as a man, beamed down from heaven as it were, and walked among people for three years may be tolerable, even if far-fetched. But the idea of God as the helpless babe of Bethlehem? That's stretching it! But consider: Had God's purpose been only to provide salvation for us, Jesus could have appeared as a man and accomplished his work on the cross; had God's purpose been simply to model righteousness for us, Jesus could have appeared as a man and revealed it by his manner of life. Yet there was more to Christ's coming than saving us or showing us how to live, as gracious as that was.

When I was a boy, baseball was my favorite pastime. I grew up in the heyday of the Los Angeles Dodgers, when Maury Wills was stealing more than one hundred bases in a season and Sandy Koufax was their ace on the mound. I wanted to be like them. By the hour, I would throw the baseball against the cement block wall in our backyard, pretending to be a star pitcher. As my indulgence became a fixation, I wanted to get my own baseball glove. My dad saw to it that I got one. But as grateful as I was that my dad had provided the means for me to play baseball, I was much happier when he picked up his own glove and said, "Let's go play baseball together." The fact that Dad bought me a glove and a baseball was his way of saying, "Son, I'm for you—have a good time." But when he said, "Let's do it together," it was as if Dad was saying, "I'm not just for your playing—I want to be with you."

When God took the form of a baby boy, it was as if he was saying, "Let's do it together." It was not enough for God to be *for* us; he wanted to be *with* us. He became, through his Son, *Immanuel—God with us.*

The fact that deity became a baby points to one of the most profound truths in the entire plan of God. In becoming a baby and growing up as we do, Jesus felt everything we feel; he was tempted and tested even as we are so that he could empathize with our weakness. But why? So that he could, in a sense, earn the right to walk into your life, put his Spirit into your body, and live his life through you.

The apostle Paul exclaimed, "If God is for us, who can be against us?" Christ's death and resurrection were God's way of declaring that he was for us. It is what theologians call the *Atonement*—Christ died for us to save us. For what greater expression of God being "for us" could we ask? And yet God in his great big Father-heart of love said, "It is not enough that I'm *for* you—I want to be *with* you." *Immanuel.*

The Atonement saved us; the Incarnation raised us. What I mean by that is this: The fact that Jesus died for us is overwhelming. We who are the recipients of such grace could live forever as grateful servants in inextinguishable ecstasy. But it was not enough for God to create grateful servants—he wanted children. And that's why deity became a seven-and-a-half-pound baby boy. By going through everything we'll ever go through and now living his life through us—responding to our every challenge, our every weakness with the power and grace he drew from the Spirit while on earth—the Lord is bringing us to maturity as sons and daughters.

Had Jesus not become a baby, he could not have entered into our lives. Remember, it's "Christ *in* you" that is your hope of glory. Our calling is not just to *imitate* Christ, but to *yield* to Christ and let him live his life through us. He's already endured every hardship you'll ever face and every temptation you'll ever encounter. Next time somebody provokes you to anger, don't try to get over your anger. Allow the Lord to respond to that anger through you the way he did when he was on the earth—by drawing on the power of the Holy Spirit. Next time you feel worry welling up inside, don't fret yourself into a fit. Simply say, "Lord Jesus, you've already confronted this kind of worry when you were a man. I'm sure the circumstances were different, but the root causes were just the same. Therefore, Jesus, respond through me right here, right now, the way you responded to this kind of worry while you were on the earth. For I believe that you are in me, and I now yield myself to you that you might respond through me."

I wish I could talk to Joan Osborne. I wish I could tell her that God *did* become one of us and that he needn't be a stranger, but the closest friend she could ever know. And he's not trying to find his way home. No, he's already made a home—for all who will yield to his love.

Lord, I've thanked you before—but I thank you again for the
fact that everything I have ever gone through,
every hurt I have ever felt, and every challenge
I have ever faced you have already experienced.

Thank you for becoming not just a man, but a baby.
Thank you for becoming helpless so that I could be helped.
Thank you for being willing to grow as a man
so that I might grow as your child.
And help me to see every difficulty I face as an opportunity to
let your life and power well up within me in response.
I can look forward to difficulties because they give
me a chance to partner with you as I
watch you overcome them through me.

QUESTIONS TO PONDER:

1. What does it mean to your relationship with God to know that he, having become a man through the person of Jesus Christ, understands your struggles?

2. In what ways do you believe your relationship with God would be different had he *not* become a man?

3. Does it give you strength to know that Jesus, like us, was tempted, yet remained sinless?

4. Is it difficult for you to believe God wants to be *with* you?

Chapter 10

WHEN HE BECAME SIN

God made him who had no sin to be sin.
2 CORINTHIANS 5:21

I once had a friend who was gay. His name was Darryl, and though he came from a Christian background, he lived a gay lifestyle for a number of years. One day, God's love reached out to him again, and he found Christ in a new and living way. He forsook his lifestyle, began attending a Bible-believing church, and grew in his relationship with the Lord.

For a couple of years the genuineness of his faith and maturity of his walk were evident to all—until the day he met rejection at the hands of someone very dear to him. It was a rejection that devastated him to the point that he felt he could find solace only in the lifestyle he had forsaken. He returned to the gay community, pursuing the companionship that seemed to him his only assurance of some whiff of acceptance.

All the while, though, Darryl wrestled inside with what he knew was wrong. Still, the pain of the rejection had been so intense that he felt Jesus couldn't relate to him; that Jesus couldn't touch him where he needed it most.

Somehow, some way, Jesus did touch Darryl, and he found his way back to the Lord. But shortly after he recommitted his life to Christ, he discovered he had AIDS. After all he'd been through, now this. He felt utterly numbed by hopelessness. But he didn't blame God or turn his back on him. Instead, as the disease began to ravage his body, he took it upon himself to share the love of Christ with all he met—his doctors, the nurses in the hospital, his friends. For over a year he struggled with the disease. Then he realized that his life was quickly coming to an end. Still, he was satisfied knowing that he had lived victoriously for Jesus in a body riddled with pain.

On what turned out to be his last day of life, a friend of his came to visit him in the hospital. As this friend approached the door of his room, he peeked through the window and noticed that Darryl was sitting upright in his bed, talking excitedly to someone his friend couldn't see through the window. As he looked closer, trying to catch a glimpse of Darryl's mysterious visitor, he noticed at the foot of the bed a large, glowing light, but he still could see no person in that room. This friend looked in absolute amazement, for Darryl appeared to be talking in animated fashion with—a light? What could it be? An angel, perhaps?

No—Jesus was in that room. Jesus was succoring an AIDS patient, preparing to take him home. Jesus could be in that room with Darryl because, you see, Jesus *had* been an AIDS patient. He knew exactly what Darryl was feeling, what he had gone through, and the depths of sin to which he had plunged. But because Jesus had become sin on the cross, he was fully able to identify with Darryl as he lay dying on that bed.

This is, perhaps, one of the most profound mysteries of the Cross. For Christ, the Cross meant ultimate identification with us. The agony he went through was far deeper than merely "carrying our sin" as a legal substitute. Paul says in 2 Corinthians that Jesus *became* sin. In that moment of supreme agony, he knew what it was like to be a thief, an addict, an outcast; he came face-to-face with all that has ever been evil. Not that he chose to become these things, for he was on that cross out of obedience to his Father. But neither did he simply die a contractual death quite removed from any sense of our depravity.

He *felt* what it was like to be a drunken outcast in a slum's gutter.

He *felt* the misery of a broken marriage.

He *felt* the dread of an anxiety-ridden student.

He *felt* the raw dependence of an addict looking for his next fix.

He *felt* the shame of the prostitute aching over her lost innocence, wishing she could be a little girl again.

In this sense, he *became* sin.

It is easy for people to point to Jesus and say, "How can you ever identify with my pain and brokenness, since you never sinned?" In response to that question, a wise old preacher once said, "What Jesus didn't feel in his life, he felt in his death." We've all had experiences where intense frustration sends us over the edge, provoking us to spew a variety of colorful metaphors into the air. And then we say to ourselves, "How can God ever identify with me? Jesus never swore!" Ah, but that's where we're wrong. Jesus has felt not only the spectrum of human emotions, but also the loss and the guilt of sin. He has *felt* the emotional residue of the man who, having cursed and blasphemed, feels ashamed and miserable. There's not a human emotion—good or bad—that Jesus did not feel. He became sin. On that cross, every perverse thought ever thought and every selfish act ever committed was poured into Christ until his heart literally broke under the strain.

The Cross wasn't simply a rehearsed script. When Jesus cried out, "My God, my God, why have you forsaken me?" he wasn't just quoting the twenty-second Psalm in order to fulfill prophecy. He was genuinely expressing shock to a Father who himself was facing a new horror: separation from his beloved Son.

We are so suspicious of emotion that we tend to regard God as a supermind, running like an atomic timepiece. Yet when we remove true emotion from God's nature, we are bound to trivialize the way he works. The trauma of Calvary goes well beyond Christ's physical agony. For the Son of God to ask his Father "Why?" reveals a depth of anguish never plumbed by human understanding. For Deity to ask Deity "Why?" certainly must have split eternity.

How could this be? Lest we become too smug with easy answers, it is said that Martin Luther sat and fasted for days to find an answer to this deepest of mysteries and found none. All we can do is stand in amazement at a God who endured so much for us.

The ultimate question people ask of God is "Why?" Why was I

born this way? Why did this happen? Why have I suffered so? Yet Christ has been there, driven to a desperation that made him cry "Why?"—identifying with us totally so that we can be totally free.

If we ever find ourselves spiritually apathetic, there's no greater cure than a good hard look at the Cross.

Lord Jesus, when I consider the immensity of love
revealed in the cross upon which you bore my
sin and sorrows, I am overwhelmed by grace's sweet mystery.
That you have felt my frustrations and tasted my weaknesses
is one thing; that you became my vileness is quite another.
I wait in your presence, stunned by the thought
of the depths to which you plunged to rescue me.
It has been said, Lord, that there is no spiritual ill
that cannot be healed by a long, hard look at the Cross.
Brand my heart with the thought of it!
Pierce my heart as your side was pierced;
penetrate my mind as the thorns dug deep into your brow.
Never let me forget the Cross—
for it is to me the wellspring of worship's flow.

QUESTIONS TO PONDER:

1. What does it mean to you that Jesus Christ actually *became* sin and that God had to turn his back on his only Son?

2. What do you believe must have happened to the Father and Son's hearts and emotions at the moment God forsook Jesus Christ?

3. Do you see Jesus as one who totally understands your pain and brokenness? Why or why not?

4. What is our appropriate response to God's free offer of forgiveness? How does that offer change how we live?

Chapter 11

A GOD WHO GRIEVES

"My people, what have I done to you?
How have I burdened you?"
MICAH 6:3

There is an interesting anecdote about Dr. Samuel Johnson, the renowned English essayist of the eighteenth century. He had just finished the last piece for his dictionary, which had been delayed numerous times. He gave the final copy to a boy who then delivered it to the printer. Upon the boy's return, Dr. Johnson asked him, "Well, boy, and what did he say to you?" The boy replied, "He said, sir, 'Thank God I have done with him.'" To that, Johnson commented, "I am glad that he thanks God for anything."

It is true enough that for many, "God" is just an exclamatory filling for expressions of disgust. Most of us just don't have time to cultivate a relationship with God, nor do we fully realize how much he wants to have a relationship with us. And yet his desire for a relationship with you and me runs deeper than our deepest longings.

Have you ever cared for someone so deeply that you wanted to give and give to them, expecting nothing in return but the sheer joy of knowing they're receiving your love? Have you ever felt the pain of wanting so desperately to give love to that someone, only to have them thanklessly demand more—or spurn it altogether?

Most of us have known the anguish of rejected love. But have we ever thought that God feels anguish—anguish infinitely beyond anything we could imagine—when his love is rejected? What must God feel like when millions of people a day shake their fist at him, curse his name, or simply ignore him? How must it grieve the God of supreme love when he is accused of being indifferent and uncaring, even calloused and cruel?

We never think that there is a part of God that grieves, and grieves deeply. We just assume that God has got it all together and that he is big enough to do what he wants to do when he wants to do it and that he puts up with that stuff, knowing he will be vindicated in the end. Yes, he can do what he wants to do when he wants to do it, but that doesn't mean he is not moved to real anguish over the blindness into which humankind has fallen. His love is not only pure unselfishness, but also deep affection. God's heart can be delighted, but it can also be broken.

When we read of Jeremiah mourning for his people, can we not look past the prophet and see the very heart of God when he cries out, "Oh, that my head were a spring of water and my eyes a fountain of tears! I would weep day and night for…my people"

(Jeremiah 9:1)? Can we not sense the hurt of God's heart when he plaintively pleads, "My people, what have I done to you? How have I burdened you?" (Micah 6:3). Can we not feel the pain of a God searching for the reason his people ignore his tender affections and protective love? Can we not sense the disconsolation in God as he looks for some way to connect with those who have rejected his love?

Yes, God has it all together. He has it so together that his love is perfect, and when that love is rejected, his grief is unfathomable.

When God the Father made our first parents, he not only desired to love them, but he also wanted them to share in something. From the beginning, it was God's desire to bring the entire universe under the lordship of Jesus. In fact, it was designed to be a love gift to his Son. In the greatness of his love, the Father wanted all people everywhere to share in that gift. In the giving of this little planet to Christ, God wanted the joy of partnering with the very ones he created. Even in that partnership, God did not force people to a task, but strove to woo them by unconditionally giving himself.

Tragically, man and woman's desire to be like God on their own terms, in their own way, broke God's heart. Why? Because of personal offense? No, because of the relationship that was lost. Grief is proportionate to intimacy. God gave freely to the people he had created and was rejected by them. In the light of such love, can we not see how truly insane is our sin and selfishness?

God gave himself to man, and man was not satisfied.

First, God gave himself to man by trusting him with his creation; and man was not satisfied, for he wanted the fruit of one tree.

Then God gave himself to man by walking with him; and man was not satisfied, for he wanted greater power.

God gave himself to man by joining himself to man in covenant; and man was not satisfied, for he wanted a security that he could see.

God gave himself to man by speaking his word; and man was not satisfied, for he wanted a sign.

Man wanted to be God! God desired to make man happy—but God cannot create God, so it was impossible to fulfill man's wishes. Yet God so desired to make man happy that he did the next best thing: He became man and gave himself one more time. And man was not satisfied...so he killed him.

Often, unbelievers don't understand exactly why Jesus died on the cross. When told that Jesus died for them, they're bewildered. "I'm not a bad person," they say. "At least, I'm not as bad as the next guy. After all, I try to do my best. Why would Jesus have to die on my account?" Such responses reveal just how unaware we are of our own corruption.

Novelist Joseph Conrad recognized this fact far more than most. In response to the famed philosopher Bertrand Russell, a champion of the humanist agenda, Conrad asserted, "I have never been able to find in any man's book or any man's talk anything convincing enough to stand up for a moment against my deepseated sense of fatality governing this man-inhabited world.... The only remedy for...us is a change of heart. But looking at the history of the last two thousand years, there is not much reason to expect that thing, even if man has taken to flying... Man doesn't fly like an eagle; he flies like a beetle."

Knowing just how much of a beetle I am, I have no problem understanding the necessity of the Cross when I see what sin has done to God—a God who only wanted to give himself to us and whose call to obedience is based solely on his knowledge that we will survive only if we give ourselves to him, the greatest in all existence. When I see what my selfishness has done—break God's heart, hurt other people, and contribute to the ugly tarnishing of his world—I have no problem in declaring unequivocally that I deserve to die.

For all our talk today about our need for self-esteem, it is ironic that the first step to a genuine sense of self-worth is to understand that we deserve to die. But unless we come to the place where we have grasped this essential fact, we will never truly value the work of the Cross. And if we don't value what Jesus did for us on that cross, we will never fully yield to him. If we never yield to him, we will not want to make joyful obedience a lifestyle. Thus, we will never give God a chance to put the broken pieces of our life back together and make us new people.

In his book *Beyond Humiliation,* J. George Mantle says, "Our deepest self is revealed by our attitude toward the Cross."[3] Only when we see what sin has done to the heart of God can we be truly grateful for God's ultimate sacrifice. And yet even here at the Cross, we find love's amazing power. In the words of Floyd McClung, "God used men's cruelty as the source of their forgiveness."

Those of us who claim a relationship with the Lord will no doubt deny any outright rejection of his love. We would never shake our fist in God's face, and we would never accuse him of not loving us. But lest we exclude ourselves too quickly from the ranks of those who have broken God's heart, we would be wise to remember the more subtle ways in which we vent our anger at him.

I would never accuse God directly, but I have found times when giving in to frustration—and expressing it in no uncertain terms—was, in fact, a roundabout way of accusing God. Feeling that I wasn't getting the answers I needed, I would sometimes find myself getting frustrated with my kids, with my responsibilities, and with life in general. I felt that if God just saw how frustrated I was, he would rush to my aid and give me some answers. Such outbursts of frustration can be an indirect way of rejecting God's love.

Self-pity can be another way we reject God's love. I'll never forget that as a young boy of eight I flagrantly disobeyed my father and found myself standing before him. Just as he began to mete out the appropriate discipline, I said to him, "Dad, you don't really love me." I can remember him stopping in midsentence, looking downright despondent, his eyes welling up with tears. He simply looked away and quietly asked me to leave the room. I listened at the door and heard him weep. Though I felt sorry for having hurt my dad, at least I didn't get a licking. I had felt sorry for myself and accused my dad of not loving me. My manipulation had achieved the desired goal. But I felt empty. Isn't that really what self-pity is sometimes? Isn't it our subconscious attempt to manipulate God? Perhaps we feel that if he just sees how miserable we are, he'll do something about our predicament.

It is in these and other subtle ways that we can find ourselves accusing him and rejecting his love. Perhaps when we see what our selfish attitudes do to God, we will be moved to change.

The only reason we would ever accuse him of not caring for us is that we don't understand what he is doing. We want our chicken feed, when God is trying to give us eagle's wings with which to fly.

Even if you realize that you have grieved the heart of God, know that the same love that used an act of men's cruelty at the cross as the source of our forgiveness reaches out to you at the point

of your sense of shame and lifts you once again to your heavenly
Father's embrace.

Lord, I confess that there have been times,
more than I would like to remember, when I questioned you.
Times when I became frustrated with you, even angry,
silently accusing you of not loving me.
Yet when I see how your purpose has unfolded in my life over
the years, I inevitably face the marvel of how wise you are.
Wise in what you keep from me
as well as what you give to me.
In light of such wisdom, I truly feel ashamed for
those times I have vented my anger toward you.
I know that I stand forgiven in your presence because of your
wondrous work of grace, but that blessed assurance doesn't
lessen the very real sorrow I feel when I view your patient love
against the backdrop of my impatience and frustration.
Give me eyes to see what you
are doing even when I don't understand.
Help me to trust you.
Help me to remember that your invitation to trust means that
there's something I'm not seeing and that because it is you who
invites, whatever I'm not seeing has got to be good!

QUESTIONS TO PONDER:

1. What things do people do that grieve God?

2. Does it seem contradictory to you that an all-powerful God can grieve? Why?

3. On what terms does God seek a relationship with us?

4. In what ways do we accuse or question God?

Chapter 12

THE ANGER
OF GOD

The LORD'S anger burned against Moses.
EXODUS 4:14

Who among us has not blown a fuse when some local yokel has pulled in front of us in the fast lane going thirty-five miles per hour? Who among us has not been seized with wild paroxysms of frustration when we have had to explain something important to a desk jockey for the tenth time, and they still don't get it? Or what about the times when you're shuttled from office to office to office in search of one simple little answer to one simple little question? These kinds of things are enough to make the coolest customer erupt in conniptions.

Psychologists tell us that one of the primary reasons we become angry is our perception that our goals are being blocked. Whether it's the promotion we think we deserve or the theater seat we're scrambling for, if someone gets in our way, we get mad. Somebody pushes us one step too far, or someone irritates us, or another's incompetence frustrates us, and we're steamed.

Naturally when we read of God's anger toward Moses, we view it through the lens of our own experiences. "Moses tried God's patience," we say; "He pushed God just one step too far." We believe that God finally became perturbed by Moses' stubbornness, and the burning bush heated up.

The thought of coming face-to-face with God's anger generally turns our spines to jelly. Images of fire falling and the earth opening up have a way of arresting our attention. Most of us are scared spitless of God's anger—probably because of the way we perceive anger in the first place. We tend to read our emotions into God's responses and conclude that Moses had just made God mad. After all, if someone treated us the way Moses treated God, we'd tell that person where he could get off. But is this an accurate understanding of God's anger?

God was calling Moses to a glorious purpose. He knew things Moses didn't. He saw a future destiny that few people in history would ever glimpse. He saw Moses confronting the most powerful man in the world; he saw Moses parting seas and bringing water out of rocks; he knew that one day Moses would stand face-to-face with him on a mountain and receive a law that would become foundational to civilization itself. Few men would ever know the thrill and privilege Moses would know. Yet in the face of inexpressible glory, Moses was incredulously obtuse, throwing back at God all the reasons why his involvement in the divine plan wasn't such a good idea.

One by one, God patiently deflected all of Moses' excuses. Finally Moses got honest and said to God, "Send somebody else to deliver your people." The only response God had left that could preserve Moses' future was his anger. So he demonstrated it in explosive fashion—his anger burned.

But we must understand that God wasn't angry *at* Moses—he was angry *for* Moses. His was not the wrath of an indignant monarch, but the intensity of a loving God. He did not want Moses to miss such a destiny. So rather than leave Moses to his mediocre existence, he flashed his anger in an attempt to jolt Moses into obedience. It was not because God was so egocentric that he wanted his will done at all costs, but because he cared enough for Moses not to let him miss this opportunity.

The anger of the Lord is not to be avoided; it is to be embraced, for it is God's protective love in action. He doesn't get angry *at* us— not in the way we humans understand anger—but *for* us because he doesn't want us to miss his best. God is slow to anger and possesses patience beyond our comprehension. But if, through our obstinacy or neglect, we fail to apprehend the wonderful design God has for our lives, and if the only response that God has left is his anger as a means of spurring us to action, then let us receive it gladly and respond appropriately, because it is a sure sign of his love. God's anger may startle us, but his indifference would devastate us.

Moses encountered God's anger again a little later in the story, where Scripture says simply that God met Moses on his way to Egypt and was about to kill him (Exodus 4:24). Now, how in the world can you figure that one? Moses was finally being obedient to the will of God, and God wanted to kill him. Not much explanation is given except that after his encounter with God, Moses immediately circumcised his son. This might be the clue that unlocks what seems to be a very puzzling response on God's part.

Four centuries earlier, God had made a covenant with Moses' ancestor, Abraham. It was a promise of unparalleled blessing. But the sign of the covenant was circumcision. Every male of Abraham's descendants was to be circumcised—an interesting sign, to say the least. (Next time we ask God for a sign, we would be wise to think twice.) This rite of circumcision was the key that was to release God's blessing to each subsequent generation. Of course, this foreshadowed the "circumcision of the heart," when a person submits his or her life to the Lord Jesus Christ and receives the indwelling power of the Holy Spirit.

As much as God wanted to bless every generation of Abraham's descendants, unless they fulfilled their part of the covenant by circumcising every male child, they could not receive his blessing. It is the same today. God wants to release a blessing on every person in the world, but only those who have been circumcised in heart by being born anew of the Spirit are included in his covenant and are thus in a place to receive those blessings.

The fact that Moses had neglected to circumcise his son was the reason for God's response here. But again, it was not the reaction of a king frustrated with a thick-headed servant; it was love's protection at its highest. I suggest that if Moses had gone to Egypt without having circumcised his son, God could not have released the blessing on Moses' ministry, nor demonstrated his miraculous signs. It was not because he wouldn't have wanted to, but because he could not deny his own word. Had Moses attempted any miraculous sign without that step of obedience, it would have been disastrous. He would have thrown his rod down and it would have remained a rod, and the people of Israel would have stoned him as a false prophet. So rather than leave Moses to the stones of an unbelieving nation, God met him at the inn and said in his big, merciful heart, "I'll just have to take you home to be with me." This was not a vengeful deity accosting Moses, but a Father of love!

All this is not meant to romanticize God's anger: He is still the God who sent the flood, the God who summoned the earth to swallow the malcontent Korah and his followers in Moses' day, and, yes, the God who, having given a new covenant of grace, did not hesitate to strike down Ananias and Sapphira for lying to the Holy Spirit. But we must see the anger of the Lord through the lens of love. Had he not sent the flood, people would have ultimately destroyed each other through their vices; it was love that caused the flood and rescued Noah's family in order to begin anew. His wrath is the means by which he radically checks the onslaught of selfishness. A. W. Tozer puts it this way: "Every wrath and judgment in the history of the world has been a holy act of preservation."[4] Though it may not always appear to be so, everything God does can be explained in terms of his love.

Those of us who are his children need never dread his hints of anger. It is but another facet of his incomprehensible love. And if we can't always be led by his tenderness, let's be grateful that he loves us enough to jar us by his anger to the place where we are walking in our destiny and satisfied by his affections.

I embrace all of the expressions of your love—
including your anger.
It actually makes me feel secure
that you love me enough to get angry with me,
if necessary; that you love me enough to
let me hear the sternness of your
voice and sense the agitation of your displeasure.
As a preacher once said, "You're out to do me good!"
So, lead on, O Lord!
And help me to remember that your
anger is indeed your protective love in action.

QUESTIONS TO PONDER:

1. How is God's anger different from our own?

2. What sorts of things make God angry?

3. Have you ever felt the anger of God?

4. What is our appropriate response to God's anger?

Chapter 13

MISUNDERSTANDING GOD

The LORD descended to the top of Mount Sinai and…
when the people saw the thunder and lightning and heard the trumpet
and saw the mountain in smoke, they trembled with fear…
and said to Moses, "Speak to us yourself and we will listen.
But do not have God speak to us or we will die."
Moses said to the people, "Do not be afraid. God has come to test you,
so that the fear of God will be with you to keep you from sinning."
EXODUS 19:20; 20:18–20

ruce Shelly, senior professor of church history at Denver Theological Seminary, told this story: "World War II was almost over. News of the armistice had reached the troops, but the actual order to cease fire was still on the way to the front. Then a bursting shell tore open a soldier's flesh. As the blood flowed out of the fatal wound, he said, 'Isn't this just like God?'"

This story could be replayed millions of times over, perhaps in lesser circumstances, but with no less sense of anger and accusation aimed at a God who many feel has dealt them a bad hand. Although his many accusers feel quite justified in shaking their fists in his face, perhaps they have completely misunderstood God.

Misunderstood him just as the Israelites had done so long ago.

For more than four hundred years, God had waited—waited to deliver his people from a cruel captivity; waited to form the greatest nation on earth from mere slaves; waited to bring his people into a land brimming with prosperity. But more than anything else, God had waited for the time when he could live among his chosen people in intimate relationship with them. I use the word *intimate* purposely, because throughout the Old Testament, God uses the picture of marriage to describe the depth of his feelings toward his people.

Jeremiah understood this quite well. In fact, the first message he preached, recorded in the second chapter of the book that bears his name, summoned the nation back to the passion of bridal affection for her God. He says, "I remember…how as a bride you loved me and followed me through the desert…" (Jeremiah 2:2).

Jeremiah is referring here to Israel's encounter with God at Mount Sinai. The scene at the foot of that mountain was explosive—fireballs from heaven, volcanic eruptions, and such. The people themselves had just gone through something of a national cataclysm. After centuries of status quo—albeit a miserable status quo—their society had been radically altered, delivered from the most powerful ruler on the face of the earth at the time. They had witnessed an unparalleled display of the supernatural and raced out of Egypt loaded with loot into an uncharted wilderness to meet a God they knew little about. All at once they found themselves ushered to the mountain to watch God breathe his law to them. And breathe he did—with fire and smoke.

Jeremiah didn't interpret this encounter as the Divine Judge forming for himself an obedient group of adulators; rather, he saw it in terms of a husband winning himself a bride. And Sinai itself was honeymoon time! It wasn't that God was trying to intimidate the people through a colossal display of power. It wasn't that God was trying to say, "You better know who's boss, and you better not get out of line; otherwise you'll see what I will do—I will consume you in a moment!"

No, it wasn't that way at all. It was, indeed, honeymoon time. I suggest that what we see in the twentieth chapter of Exodus was God readying himself for communion with his beloved—God disrobing himself, if you will—God unveiling himself to the people. It just so happens that when God shows up, he shows up in lightning bolts and thunderclaps.

But when God's people heard the trumpet blasts and saw the inferno consuming the peak, they were beside themselves with fear and cried to Moses, "We don't want a God like that! We're afraid to get close to a God like that. You be the mediator between us and God." Astonished, Moses quickly replied, "You don't understand what God is doing. He is revealing himself to you this way to keep you from sinning!"

Moses had become God's friend. The God of the simple burning bush before whom he had trembled just months earlier was the God he now felt quite at home with in this raging conflagration. And Moses understood something about God that the people didn't. He pleaded with the people, trying to save them from the folly of their misperceptions.

You see, God knew that the people, when they entered the

Promised Land, would encounter giants twice their size and imposing cities with walls so thick that chariots could race four abreast on top. He knew that the people would be terrified of such sights, so he said in his big Father-heart of love, *I know what I'll do. I will show them myself in all my power, in all my glory. I will show them how great I am, so that they will be so impressed with me, that the giants of the land will appear to them as mere grasshoppers!* And so God, in his big, loving heart, waited and waited for centuries until that day when he brought his people to the foot of that mountain.

I don't think we can quite comprehend the depth of God's excitement. Finally, he could reveal the fullness of himself to a people. After centuries of communing with only a few individuals every now and then, after centuries of speaking in dreams and visions, God now was ready to unveil himself. Finally, there will be people who will know him as he is and revel in the privilege of communing with their Creator at such a depth of intimacy.

And they didn't get it! They completely misunderstood God, thinking he was intimidating them with a show of force, threatening to nuke them should they get out of line. And because they misunderstood, they rejected him. Scripture does not record the sound of the divine heart breaking. The people with whom God desired intimacy spurned him. This is not to suggest that God is given to maudlin shows of emotional excess, or that he is thrown off balance by our obstinacy. It is simply to say that God is a God who feels and grieves deeply when he is denied sweet communion with his people.

Like the Israelites of old, there are many today who misunderstand God. Pressures come; curve balls are hurled; well-laid plans go screwy; and desires go unmet. Often we want to shake our fist in God's face and say, "Unfair! Why are you doing this?" Or, we may sense God putting his finger on attitudes in our lives or on little treasures we clutch, such as our reputation or pocketbook. Anger builds and we say, "This is mine, I have a right!" Or fear rises and we cry, "Don't get too close, God, for I can't bear the reality of my inadequacies." And either out of anger or fear, we run from that transparent place, that vulnerable place, that intimate place where, face-to-face and empty-handed, we encounter the fiery love of a God who wants us more than we'll ever know. We run because we don't understand him or the ways he works.

If we understood him in his unfathomable love, we would not hesitate to bury our deepest selves in his outstretched arms.

Lord, I repent of those times I have run
from you or shaken my fist in your face
because I did not understand what you were doing.
By your grace I humble myself today
and ask that you would grant me perspective
in every situation, good or bad, to see that you are
working in them all for the fulfillment of your purposes
and that in yielding to your purposes
I find the sweetest satisfactions.

QUESTIONS TO PONDER:

1. In what ways do we misunderstand God?

2. What do you think is God's response when we misunderstand him?

3. What effect on us and our relationship with God does it have when we misunderstand him?

4. How do we come to know and understand God?

Chapter 14

❦

GOD: A TRUE FRIEND

*The LORD was angry with me…and he solemnly swore
that I would not cross the Jordan and enter the good land.…*
DEUTERONOMY 4:21

The depth of a relationship—be it a marriage or a long-term friendship—can often be measured by how easily the partners can be openly honest with one another and still retain the fire of love between them. To be guarded in a relationship suggests we don't trust the other person enough to be honest. We want the relationship and don't want to jeopardize it by expressing honest feelings, even angry ones. So we tiptoe around each other's fragile emotions and never grow up as human beings. Show me a couple who can express honest displeasure in what one partner has done, yet still retain a sense of closeness and not be threatened by such expressions, and I will show you a couple who are truly, deeply in love.

God wants friends he can be direct with. There is a place in God where we are no longer intimidated by his displeasure, a place where we can receive God's anger and love him all the more.

To Moses, the disappointment of not being allowed to enter the Promised Land after forty years of tireless ministry to an ungrateful people was the most bitter of his life. In the book of Deuteronomy, which was Moses' last sermon to the people, he keeps coming back to it—in chapter 1, in chapter 3, and again in chapter 4. His repetition of that event underscores the intensity of his disappointment.

You remember the story. In Numbers, chapter 20, God told Moses to speak to the rock to provide water for the grumbling and rebellious people. This was the second time God had told Moses to use an impenetrable boulder to bring forth the liquid sustenance of life. (Of course, that's a little insight in and of itself: What seems to us to be the most impossible situation can often become the source of life to us. Such is the grace and greatness of our God. But that is going beyond our present bounds.) The issue was that God told Moses to *speak* to the rock, not strike it with the rod as he had done before. Moses, in his impatience and frustration, fell back on the strategy that had worked before and struck the rock again. God confronted Moses at that point and said, "Because you did not trust in me enough to honor me as holy in the sight of the Israelites, you will not bring this community into the land I give them" (Numbers 20:12).

The fact is, Moses did not trust God with one little detail. He struck the rock instead of speaking to it, and God became angry. It is one thing to have failed. That is emotionally damaging enough.

It is another thing to experience God's anger at our point of failure. That can be utterly devastating. It is at the point of our failure that we most covet God's redemptive grace.

But let us for a moment get beyond that one-dimensional view of God. God's anger did absolutely nothing to undermine Moses' relationship with him. The level of intimacy remained intact, such was the closeness Moses enjoyed with God. Again, Moses' receptivity to God's anger showed that he had come to a place of such intimacy that even anger was a part of the relationship. It was that place of raw honesty where sin has real consequence, yet the love level continues to grow deeper. That is the place of true friendship.

Sometimes oversensitivity is indicative of a relationship that is much too fragile. Never look at God's anger as something by which to be threatened. Instead, look at it as an indication of a deeper relationship.

The other day my wife, Nancy, and I took a drive to the Cumberland Plateau, situated on the southern border of Tennessee where it meets Georgia. It was one of those intoxicating autumn days when the rays of the sun dance on the trees and fall breezes playfully toy with the many-colored leaves; when there is a certain snap in the air, and the aroma of apples and wood smoke bathes one's senses and massages one's mind.

As we were driving, Nancy turned to me and said something simple, but quite profound. "Do you know, honey, I think I'm finally comfortable with being vulnerable."

I thought about that statement for a moment and realized that she was putting her finger on one of the most delightful fruits of maturity. She had come to the place where openness was no longer a threat, where people could more easily be direct with her without jeopardizing her sense of worth. Like many of us, she has had her share of hard knocks. But that vulnerability to which she had risen was really the result of her deepening security in God. The fact that those closest to her could be direct without feeling they were hurting her or harming their relationship suggests she had reached a major pinnacle.

So it is in our relationship with God: we can become vulnerable to his love. And as God sees that we are becoming more and more secure in his love, he can be more and more direct with us. He is infinitely patient with us as he nudges us along the path of true friendship with him. But remember, in our journey with God, we are to be, as Michael Quoist says in his book *Prayers of Life,* "very, very little, for the Father carries only little children." [5]

Lord, I want to be so close to you that even when you correct
me, I'll receive it as a treasured display of your boundless
affections. Let not my insecurities keep me from giving you the
joy of being open and direct with me, like face-to-face friends.
I don't want you to have to traipse
delicately around my fragile emotions in
your attempts to guide me in the paths of life.
I know you are patient with me—you will find
a thousand ways and more to teach me.
But by your grace, so convince me of your endless love
that I would welcome the strongest rebuke
as a token of deepest companionship.

QUESTIONS TO PONDER:

1. Is it difficult for you to think of God as your friend? Why or why not?

2. What do you think is the nature of a true friendship with God?

3. How is God's offer of friendship different from that of men?

4. How does understanding that God counts you a friend change your approach to him?

Chapter 15

〰️

OUR RIGHTEOUS JUDGE

"Will not the Judge of all the earth do right?"
GENESIS 18:25B

I was fortunate to have a great dad. He was keenly interested in me and displayed a kindness that was always endearing. He had his weaknesses, as do we all, but on the whole he was terrific.

Yet, no matter how great a father is, there is one thing he has a hard time providing: objectivity. To a good dad, his kid is always the best, whether or not it's really true. Affirmation, however inaccurate, is always a welcome elixir for our sense of inadequacy. But there are times when that is not enough. As essential as a dad's love is, it can be very subjective.

When I was sixteen, I got my first traffic ticket. I'd had my driver's license all of six months when I was nailed for a ridiculous violation. My dad and I decided to contest it in court. We won, and my manhood was restored. Now, my father could have stressed how good a driver I was in an attempt to reinforce my confidence. But that would have mattered little. At that time, I needed a judge to tell me where I stood, not just a dad to tell me I was okay. I needed a verdict, not just fatherly compassion.

God is a gracious Father. He is also an unbiased Judge. To us, that seems like "the long arm of the law" from which we'd just as soon keep a safe distance. We attach a severity to his judgments that unnerves us. Love and grace are so much more appetizing. Yet there is a wonder in his judgments that many fail to appreciate. God is indeed our Judge, but far from feeling anxious about it, we should feel secure—if we understand it. Many have rediscovered God's Fatherhood in recent years, and to those whose fathers were distant, intolerant, or even cruel, such a theme as God's fathering care needs to be stressed again and again. But as we heal up and mature, we find ourselves ready to embrace other aspects of God's character, which at first glance don't seem quite so appealing. Valuing God as our Judge marks a significant step in our spiritual growth.

God is a perfect Father *and* Judge. He not only affirms us as his children, but also tells us where we stand. What security! God as my Father summons my love; God as my Judge summons my trust. For when faced with injustice or offense, can we not agree with Abraham and say, "Shall not the judge of all the earth do right?" Can we not rest in a justice firmly based in truth, even if we find ourselves on the unpleasant side of correction? It is comforting to know that we have a God who is totally unbiased in his assessment of us.

At first, it may not seem that comforting. We might wish he would bend his justice a little in favor of his love because we don't want an accurate picture of what we are, but would prefer a computer-enhanced version that trims us where we spiritually sag. But is that love? Is it love to color the truth about us just to preserve our sense of well-being? If God were biased in his judgments, might he not also be capricious in his love? If his justice were not pure, could his love be trusted? We long for the day God says to us, "Well done"; but the one reason his evaluation will mean something is because it will be pronounced by a Judge who is utterly truthful, not just a Father who desires our happiness. It is the justice of God that validates love. Without justice, love is nothing more than sentimental romanticism. It is cheap feeling masquerading as moral substance.

Of our three kids, our youngest, Caleigh, is the pistol. Now imagine little Caleigh and me sitting in front of the television watching our beloved cartoons. I say to her, "Caleigh, Daddy is going to go into the kitchen and get us some cookies. While Daddy is gone for a minute, don't touch the television. If you disobey and touch the television, Daddy will have to spank your hand." So I go, fetch the cookies, and come back into the family room, where I find conspicuous little handprints all over the screen. The vertical is fighting the horizontal, and the cartoons we were watching are as jumbled as a Picasso painting. Obviously, little Caleigh has touched the TV.

Now at that point, there is nothing in me that wants to follow through with the discipline. I don't want to spank her hand. Yet I had given her a simple directive that was meant to ensure her happiness. I had given it so that the picture wouldn't be distorted, allowing her to continue enjoying the 'toons—but she obviously wasn't enjoying them now. If I don't follow through in keeping my word about the consequences of her behavior, how will she be able to believe in my word later on? In other words, if I don't follow through with what I've said here, how will she trust me if I promise her a trip to Disneyland? You see, love and justice are inseparable. Love and justice are two sides of the same coin.

When our first parents disobeyed the commands of the Lord, I don't think it was in the Father's heart to rush punishment. Everything within him that breathes compassion wanted to say, "It's okay; I will give you another chance. We'll forget this ever happened, and I'll disregard the consequences." This may have been God's heart, but his word was at stake. If he didn't follow through with his word then, how could anybody trust his word later? Not only that, but for God to go against his word would be tantamount to admitting a mistake—that he never should have given the command in the first place. Thus he would cease to be perfect and therefore cease to be God. He would self-annihilate, and we would all go up in a puff of smoke! Of course, one might say, "Why did he utter such an edict in the first place?" Again, to ensure the happiness of his creation. The point is that his love compels his justice. Love gave the command and love enforced the consequences when it was disobeyed.

Lord, I embrace this revelation of you.
So often I have run from it, thinking that
your role as Judge was intimidating and threatening.
But now I see it as just one more expression of your love,
which fosters within me a deep sense of security.
Because you are my Judge, you are a
compass to me as I navigate through life.
Because you are my Judge, I never have to
navigate in a fog, not knowing exactly where I stand.
Because you are my Judge, I can develop the kind of
confidence that can face life's most trying assaults and the
enemy's harshest attacks, with the jubilant bounce of faith.

QUESTIONS TO PONDER:

1. How does the thought of God as your righteous Judge affect you? Does it frighten you?

2. What is the relationship between God's judgment and his love?

3. Do you tend to welcome God's judgment or run away from it?

4. How is God's judgment different from our own?

Chapter 16

A GOD WHO STRUGGLES

How can I give you up, Israel?
How can I abandon you?…
My heart will not let me do it!
My love for you is too strong.
HOSEA 11:8, TEV

Many people have the idea that God, while benevolent and merciful, inhabits a remote region of unruffled serenity; that he is sort of a galactic Confucius, calmly stroking his antiquated beard with his antiquated fingers. Many think of him as a *que será será* God who knows that "what will be, will be" and is thus removed from any sort of struggle, forever sedated by his sovereignty. To many, ascribing to God emotions that beset us poor creatures seems perilously close to blasphemy.

Words like *restless, struggle,* or *grief* in reference to God seem at first glance irreverent and dishonoring, portraying a God of limited knowledge and short-circuited power. But God is a God who feels, and though he is unchanging and will accomplish all of his purposes, though the end of history is never in doubt as far as God is concerned, still he has his moments of grief and struggle with us.

To say that God struggles is not to say that he is uncertain about the outcome of his purposes, nor that he is driven in any way by frustrations, nor that he is ever at any time not in ultimate control of his creation. As R. C. Sproul has stated, "There is not one random atom in the universe." He is God the *Almighty,* before whose presence even the most pious come unraveled (Revelation 1:17; Isaiah 6:5). Yet raising the possibility that God does in some way struggle, we come dangerously close to perceiving God in our likeness, seeing him as a mere superman—more powerful than, but essentially like us.

To say that God struggles *is* to say that, in his very real interaction with people, he is constantly wooing us, often agonizing over us, even sometimes contending with us, all the while drawing us to himself. He is a God who, as Donald Bloesch says, "is not an Unmoved Mover but One who is restless 'until He establishes Jerusalem' (Isaiah 62:1, 7). This is a God who agonizes over His children...."[6]

To say God struggles is to see in him that gracious tenacity, so well captured by Francis Thompson in his classic ode *The Hound of Heaven,* in which the Lord says:

Human love needs human meriting:
How have you merited—of all man's clotted clay the dingiest clot?
Alas, you know not how little worthy of love you are!
Who will you find to love ignoble you, save Me?

All which I took from you I did but take, not for your harm,
    But just that you might seek it in My arms.
All which your child's mistake fancies
as lost I have stored for you at home:
Rise, clasp My hand, and come![7]

We can sense something of the God who struggles in the book of Jeremiah, where God reluctantly metes out necessary disciplines while aching for restored relationship:

"I have surely heard Ephraim's moaning: 'You disciplined me like an unruly calf, and I have been disciplined....' Is not Ephraim my dear son, the child in whom I delight? Though I often speak against him, I still remember him. Therefore my heart yearns for him; I have great compassion for him," declares the Lord. (Jeremiah 31:18, 20)

Can we not sense the pain of love's desire here? Can we not feel the churning of a Father's heart? To be sure, God moves from within his own inner peace, but that's not the same thing as passivity. We tend to confuse the two. These emotions of sorrow and disappointment don't alter God's perfect peace, nor disrupt his inner sense of composure. To say that God struggles, though, is to acknowledge that a certain kind of grief registers within him. And it is that response of grief that his perfect love and peace immediately transforms into acts of mercy toward us. The struggle is not the absence of peace as it would be with us, but rather the interplay of registering holy disappointment, even grief, with an instantaneous expression of mercy so that we might be wooed to his embrace.

Perhaps no book captures this like the book of Hosea, where God calls his prophet to marry the prostitute Gomer, as an illustration of what he has experienced repeatedly with his beloved people. Hosea endures intense anguish while his wife plies her trade in the embrace of other men. Yet his grief never once sways Hosea to abandon his God-given purpose as a prophet. This is the way it is with God. Because he is a God of justice, he must allow his people to suffer the consequences of their own choices (again, love without justice is but cheap emotion), but still he loves them:

> The Lord says, "When Israel was a child, I loved him and called him out of Egypt as my son. But the more I called to him, the more he turned away from me.... Yet I was the one who taught Israel to walk. I took my people up in my arms, but they did not acknowledge that I took care of them. I drew them to me with affection and love. I picked them up and held them to my cheek; I bent down to them and fed them. They refuse to return to me...[therefore] war will sweep through their cities and break down the city gates.... They will cry out because of the yoke that is on them, but no one will lift it from them. How can I give you up, Israel? How can I abandon you?... My heart will not let me do it! My love for you is too strong." (Hosea 11:1–8, TEV)

There is pathos here. This is not an unfeeling cosmic force, but a God who bears within himself the wounds of love's noblest expression: truth. To neglect rightness for the sake of a relationship is to ultimately erode the very foundation of that relationship; on the other hand, to enforce rightness is to risk rejection. This is the essence of the struggle. Perhaps in the end, to say that God struggles is to identify that moment when he takes grief and turns it into compassion.

Oh sweet Father! I am so bent. No matter what good I may try to do, it seems that when I trace some of my motives to their deepest essence, I find nothing but self-serving. Thank you that you care enough for me to brood over me like a mother hen would her chicks. Thank you that you pursue me, hound me, even struggle with me—to get me to that pleasant place of intimacy with you.

QUESTIONS TO PONDER:

1. What kinds of emotions, if any, do you envision God expressing?

2. What does it mean to you that God "struggles"?

3. In what ways does God "woo" people to himself?

4. What does God's struggling on our behalf say to you about the nature of his love?

Chapter 17

FACING A
JEALOUS GOD

For I, the LORD your God, am a jealous God.
EXODUS 20:5

ave you ever wanted a car that seemed to you the essence of sport and vitality? Have you ever drooled over a five-on-the-floor beckoning to you in an auto show room? Or perhaps you've been tantalized by the promises of serene skies and dazzling beaches on some island paradise.

Have you, then, wanting something so badly, ever encountered the yellow flag of the Holy Spirit within, cautioning you against buying that car or taking that dream vacation, or restraining you from an indulgence that would prove to be harmful later on? If and when that ever happens to you, it is not the Holy Spirit trying to squash the fun in life. He is actually releasing you from a mountain of potential debt that would greatly handicap your future peace. That restraining work is part of what God's jealousy is all about.

To us, the whole idea of jealousy is negative. We see jealousy as a destructive emotion. Even Solomon asked the question, "Who can stand before jealousy?" (Proverbs 27:4). So when we read that God is a jealous God, we have difficulty understanding how a God of love and holiness could express such a trait.

Jealousy speaks of a possessiveness that borders on idolatry. It is a consuming passion that is singular in focus. It seeks to obtain what it loves by whatever means possible. It is a fire unquenched, a restlessness that cannot be assuaged until what it wants is what it has. It is the relentless pursuit of desire in the face of a competing affection and it has no tolerance toward a rival vying for the same heart.

Yet, God is jealous. In the purest, most relentless way, God is jealous. Does this mean he is a clutching, manipulative being who dotes on the loyal, but wreaks vengeance on the careless? No, God is not whimsical. His is a jealousy that a man or a woman can never know. In fact, God is the only one who has a right to be jealous, because he is the only one who is perfect in love.

God's jealousy is not the controlling kind. On the contrary, it is a releasing kind of jealousy. Holy jealousy—God's kind of jealousy—is love tuned to its highest pitch of desire. You see, God doesn't just love you; he *wants* you. He is not moved to love you merely to maintain his own moral excellence. He has not just *chosen* you, but has *desired* you. His jealousy is the unquenched fire, the relentless pursuit, the restless passion. His jealousy is an absolute intolerance of anything that divides our affection. God does not let go—but that is the very thing that frees. It is, in Oswald Chambers' words, to be haunted by God. "To be haunted by God," he says, "is to have an effective barricade against all the onslaughts of the enemy."[8]

What an assurance it is to know that God doesn't sit passively aside as we flirt with diversions that can so thoroughly destroy our souls, diversions such as: wanting that promotion regardless of the price; seeking that romantic relationship more than anything else; slipping into a casual sort of Christianity where we slowly cease to build our lives on the principles of his Word; or finding ourselves so disappointed that we slide into an ever-engulfing apathy.

Because of these enemies of our soul, a jealous God rushes the ramparts of our heart and demands that we yield to his love. Are these the demands of power or of a need to be served and worshiped? No. Rather, they are the demands of a God who *wants* us far more than we could ever want to be wanted and who alone is wise enough to justify those demands.

In Ephesians 4:1, Paul refers to himself as "the prisoner of the Lord." This is another one of those fabulous paradoxes that we find when we plumb the depths of the kingdom of God. For Paul, being a prisoner of the Lord was a liberating thing. Again, in Romans 1:1, Paul calls himself a devoted servant, more literally a "bondslave" to God. A bondslave was one who, after having earned his freedom, decided voluntarily to commit himself to a lifetime of servitude for the sake of his master. Even when Paul found himself a literal prisoner for the sake of the Lord, in a Roman cell or a Philippian jail, it was still freedom to him—for freedom to Paul was not avoiding the restraints of the Holy Spirit, but joyfully accepting them. The restraining ministry of the Holy Spirit is a grace, not a bondage. When the Holy Spirit restrains us, he is not controlling us, but, in fact, releasing us. For in the restraint he is surely protecting us from a harm we cannot see as we blindly pursue our own direction.

I can recall so many times when I wanted to seize an opportunity that would certainly have advanced my career, only to feel the hot jealousy of God bearing down on my impudent will. Was the Lord trying to control me? Or did he see in me a root of self-seeking that, left unchecked, would most surely cause me years of misery undoing the damage that my zealous arrogance and presumption had caused?

Whenever the Lord restrains, he is actually enfolding you in his protective embrace, not keeping you from what will bring you happiness. His control is really his release in disguise.

Lord, let the fire of your jealousy blaze deep within me.
I invite the restraining work of the Holy Spirit in my life.
I accept joyfully the boundaries and limits you place upon me.
I am so grateful that you are not an indifferent God.
I am so grateful that your love is
not the passive show of an ambivalent potentate.
Oh jealous God, you will have me,
and I am mesmerized by such love!

QUESTIONS TO PONDER:

1. How is God's jealousy different from what we perceive as jealousy?

2. Why would God be jealous for us?

3. What sorts of things do we do to incur God's jealousy?

4. What is the relationship between God's jealousy and his love for us?

Chapter 18

A GOD OF HOLINESS

Worship the LORD in the beauty of holiness!
1 CHRONICLES 16:29, KJV

The picture of a holy God can be unnerving to those who see his holiness only as vengeance gone ballistic. Images of fire falling from heaven, mortals melting like wax in his presence—like something from a Steven Spielberg film—ungodliness being dealt with ever-so-severely. These are often the impressions we have when we think of God's holiness.

The Bible says God is the "consuming fire" who calls us to "work out our salvation with fear and trembling." But that's only half the story. It is to the arrogant, the flippant, and the careless that

God so reveals himself. But to the tender, to the uncertain, there is a wonderfully appealing side to his holiness.

King David's summons to "worship the Lord in the beauty of holiness," has always sounded pretty contradictory to me. I mean, how can holiness and beauty be connected in the same sentence? The holiness of God suggests to me everything that he is and everything I'm not. It suggests the depth of my lack, the extremity of my insecurity, the sense of being overwhelmed by my ineptitude and failure. When I think of things beautiful, I think of the grandeur of Yosemite Valley, the crystal-like sand of a Florida beach, or the face of my wife, Nancy, who is a very lovely woman, indeed. When I think of the word *beauty,* I certainly don't associate it with the word *holy.* So what does David know that I don't? He must have understood something about the holiness of God that, to him, made it intensely attractive.

Not too long ago, a preacher who was graciously calling us to lead holy lives challenged me. Far from the "hellfire and brimstone" image that such messages can convey, there was something fresh in his words. I responded in prayer and was enveloped in a sense of God's holy presence. It was one of those unusual encounters where the reality of God was more pronounced than everything else around me. For several moments I was captivated by his presence. My mind couldn't have wandered had I wanted it to. As I reflected on the wonder of God, I suddenly found myself responding not to an inner sense of peace, nor to some ecstatic feeling of joy, but rather to *the sheer pleasure of being enveloped in holiness.* I discovered what Jonathan Edwards, the preeminent theologian of the First Great Awakening, knew when he said, "Holiness appeared to me to be of a sweet, pleasant, charming, serene, calm nature—which brought an inexpressible purity, brightness, peacefulness, and rav-ishment to the soul."[9]

I had never quite seen God's holiness in that light. I said to myself, "I am actually enjoying the presence of a holy God." It was like the feeling of a hot shower after a sweaty day of work—soap-ing down, then letting the water splash your face, rinsing you from head to foot, leaving you refreshed and clean. "The fear of the Lord is clean," David said in the nineteenth Psalm; it was a feeling of being clean, and oh, how enjoyable it was!

Holiness is intensely satisfying because it is the way of life for which we are designed. For example, we say to those seeking truth that there is a God-shaped vacuum in their lives that only he can fill and that once they yield their lives to Christ, they will know a satisfaction they've never had before. But do we believe that our-selves?

The Spirit of God who fills that vacuum is a *Holy* Spirit, and if we're designed for God—and we are—there must be something downright *enjoyable* about holiness. When we lose our desire to be holy as he is holy, we also lose that satisfying sense of being clean. To put it another way, if a life of holiness fulfills our basic design, then holiness is "coming home."

Believe it or not, one of the most interesting insights into holi-ness I've ever received came from a brief episode in a Hollywood flick. One rarely finds much, if any, spiritual merit from Tinseltown, but in this instance the screenwriter caught something. A few years ago, somebody suggested to me that I see the movie *City Slickers*. The movie (which, by the way, I'm not necessarily suggesting should be seen for its particular wealth of spiritual truths) is about three men going through midlife crises. I don't know why my friends thought it so important for me to see a movie about men going through midlife crises, but it was actually pretty entertaining.

To find themselves, these men decided to go on a cattle drive together. Embarking for points west, they encounter a grizzled old cowboy named Curly, marvelously played by Jack Palance. In the particular scene to which I am referring, one of the guys, played by Billy Crystal, joins Curly in searching for a stray calf. During the search, the Billy Crystal character asks him for the secret of life. Curly shifts in his saddle, shoves his cigarette to the side of his mouth, and, straightening his back and narrowing his eyes, lifts up one finger and says, "One thing."

One thing. That really is what the life of holiness is all about. It is being utterly and completely reduced to one thing, and where holiness is concerned, that one thing is being completely given over to God so that he might manifest his character through us. Being reduced to one thing is not only appealing, but incredibly freeing, for then we are no longer:

- a prisoner of people's expectations;
- drawn and quartered by competing desires;
- subduing unseemly motivations lurking in our souls;
- torn between success and goodness.

We are really and truly free. That's what makes holiness attractive.

To the Hebrew mind, holiness must have had some attraction to it because in the Old Testament that which was designated as holy was often something the people actually coveted. The anointing oil, for example, was so aromatic that God had to establish strict prohibitions against illicit attempts to copy it. The priesthood, also designated holy, was a snare to a king by the name of Uzziah, who so wanted to be a holy priest that he stepped over the boundaries of his own calling and ended up getting a bad case of skin rash (2 Chronicles 26:19–21).

That which was holy was regarded as something unique and special to the Hebrew. Today, God wants us to recover that sense of awe and desire that holiness was intended to excite.

The very fact that in the Old Testament the word *holy* is often associated with stuff like oil, tables, and even dirt—ordinary stuff made extraordinary because God chose it for his purposes—is a key unlocking for us a fresh perspective on holiness that may motivate us to embrace it.

When God met Moses at the burning bush, he commanded him, "Take off your sandals, for the place where you are standing is holy ground" (Exodus 3:5). Used here, the word suggests that which is completely devoted to or wholly given over to God.

Seems simple enough: We belong to him; we are hardwired to God. But somewhere we've confused the issue a bit. We've gotten the idea that holiness is just another word for righteousness. Holiness has come to mean purity of life. Which is true, as far as it goes. In fact, this idea of holiness is strongly underscored in the New Testament. We would gravely compromise our understanding of holiness if we diluted this emphasis. Still, righteousness is but one aspect of genuine holiness. If temple furniture and priestly vestments (which obviously have no ability to make moral choices) are considered holy, then holiness must be simpler and more enjoyable to walk in than a comprehensive code of conduct. Truth is, once we understand holiness, we'll desire it and come to see righteousness not so much as the result of rigorous discipline, but as the overflow of holiness.

It is intriguing that in this burning bush encounter we discover a richer revelation of holiness. Up to now, the word *holy* had been used in Scripture only once—when God created the seventh day and called it "holy" (Genesis 2:3). It is in this setting, I suggest, that the Holy Spirit chooses to enlarge our understanding of its scope and intent. The picture is a rather serene one—Moses tending sheep in the quiet solitude of the desert. In the distance, he sees a glowing bush, and as he gets closer to it, he realizes that the bush is on fire. So he gets a little closer and discovers that though the bush is on fire, the leaves are not consumed. This would have spooked many others, but something compelled Moses to draw even nearer, and as he did so, the bush talked.

Talking bushes are not the norm in the wilderness. But the moment that voice sounded from the bush, Moses knew that he was coming face to face with the Almighty. And that was when he heard the command. "Take off your sandals, Moses," God said, "for the place where you are standing is holy ground."

To get the full import of this, consider the background: God's people had been in bondage for more than four hundred years, and he desperately wanted to set them free. Now is the time for his chosen deliverer, Moses, to be summoned. But, before he can free the people, God needs to free Moses. So in his rich Father-heart of love God says, *"How can I set Moses free from all his insecurities? Ah, I know what I'll do—I will reveal my holiness to him!"* So God shows up in a burning bush, the perfect illustration of holiness.

Of course, when we view this scene through eyes that have been conditioned to fear the Father as some overbearing ogre, we tend to see only the fire and not the fact that though the bush was burning, it was not only *not* destroyed, but was actually *enhanced*, so that even insecure Moses was riveted to its glow. The point of the whole context here is freedom. And this suggests one of the most powerful truths about holiness: *Understanding holiness is the key to freedom.* And isn't that the life we crave?

The burning bush is the perfect picture of freedom. It's completely given over to God. So, as they say in the Land Down Under, "No worries." The life wholly given over to God is:

- a life free from all but the one thing;
- a life free from worry about one's needs and desires;
- a life abandoned to his care;
- a life not only not destroyed, but actually enhanced to be all that God designed it to be.

Being completely given over to God is ultimate freedom. It is the life completely abandoned to one thing: allowing God's character to be demonstrated and manifest through it. When God says, "Be holy, for I am holy," he is calling us to let him do through us what he does in and of himself—God is absolutely abandoned to manifesting the beauty of his character.

This is not heady arrogance or egocentrism on God's part, for the essence of God, as we've already seen, is that he always selflessly gives. That's what makes him the perfection and epitome of goodness. Holiness is his eternal choice to manifest that pristine character.

He calls us to no less: "Be holy for I am holy." That is not a decree to submit to a thousand do's and don'ts, but rather a clear call to make the simple, ultimate choice of abandoning ourselves to that one purpose: to let God be God through us; to be the burning bush that, by his power and grace, is effectively engulfed by the flames of holiness, yet finds itself released. No hidden agendas, no ulterior motives, no secret desires of wanting to be recognized or to accomplish greatness—just us, engulfed by the fire of God, utterly dependent, yet radically free. For in fact, when God calls us to a life wholly given over to him, he is calling us to affirm what is already a reality. For are we not already totally dependent on him for every breath we take, every talent we cultivate, every goal we achieve?

Still, our reticence to embrace holiness runs deep. It's like trying to run a moral marathon when you know good and well you'll never get beyond a hundred yards. We're discouraged before we start. And calls to be holy often just reinforce our sense that we're fighting a losing battle, leaving us more insecure than before. Of course, the only thing worse than insecurity is guilt—and many a sermon has been preached spurring people to holiness by playing off their sense of deserved condemnation.

Texts like Philippians 2:12, where Paul summons us to work out our salvation with fear and trembling, are handy indeed when it comes to shaping the behaviors of struggling saints. But look more closely. Paul's injunction is not given in the sense of being wary of a God who anxiously waits to pounce on the slightest sign of transgression. Consider the context. Paul had just written in enraptured fashion of the Christ who became a servant, the Christ obedient unto death, the Christ who is highly exalted and at whose name every knee shall one day bow. In the light of the wonder of Jesus Christ, Paul is telling us to work out our salvation with a trembling that is not the result of insecurity, but rather of the excitement of who he is, of the fear of grieving a God so wonderful, and of the joy of watching this same Jesus doing his work in us.

It is the trembling a diamond cutter knows when he examines a rare and precious gem. It is the trembling a nuclear physicist knows when he handles volatile material, rightly wary of its awesome power, but more excited about its incredible potential. It is the trembling of the adventurer who has unlocked an ancient treasure trove, rather than the trembling of a frightened child before the old schoolmaster's paddle.

Lord, open my spiritual eyes to see this most central of all
your attributes. Help me to grow in the understanding that
your holiness is absolutely beautiful and that as I pursue you,
I will find myself more and more drinking at the fountain of
eternal pleasures, which is the beauty of your holiness.
Help me to see holiness not, first and foremost,
as a set of rules that you demand I live by,
but rather as the environment I was created to enjoy.

QUESTIONS TO PONDER:

1. What does the word *holiness* mean to you?

2. Have you ever thought of God's holiness as something to be enjoyed?

3. How can you give yourself over to God's holiness?

4. What is the relationship between holiness and righteousness?

Chapter 19

HE CALLS US "HOLY"

I remember…how as a bride you loved me…
Israel was holy to the LORD.
JEREMIAH 2:2–3

Status: that highly prized commodity that excites the most intense passions in so many people. The lure of fame and the appetite for recognition drives millions of eager minds fashioned by the fantasy worlds of the silver screen and the stages of a thousand rock concerts. Feeling they have been reduced to nothing more than a statistic, many possess a need for a sense of status that is stronger than money, security, or sex. In today's world, building one's self-esteem is right up there with eating as an absolute necessity for survival.

Yet when we discover that intimate place with a holy God, something happens that cleanses us from these dominating passions and imbues us with a positive self-image anchored to a permanent source of fulfillment—a sort of "detox"—where our itch for status is satisfied in *him*. For the moment we come into relationship with God, he calls us something that expresses loudly and clearly just how special we are to God and that, when we "get it," infuses us with a sense of significance that all of Hollywood's glamour can't begin to touch.

The great, almighty Creator of all existence calls us *holy!*

"But I thought becoming holy was something you grew into; something you strove for; something you earned," some would say. Indeed, most of us perceive holiness as the unreachable domain of perfection in which God lives and for which we are destined to struggle the rest of our lives. Holiness, to us, is the top rung of maturity's ladder. But in fact, holy is something God calls us from the moment we surrender our lives to him.

In Jeremiah 2, the prophet looks back through time to the moment Israel was delivered from Egypt. Remembering the spark of bridal affections, God says of his people, "I remember how as a bride you loved me and followed me through the desert—Israel was holy to the Lord…."

Now at first sight, this passage jars our sense of fairness. We want to say, "Wait a minute, God! These Israelites had been delivered just a few days earlier and were the same Israelites who grumbled and complained even in those first few weeks in the wilderness! And yet you call them holy? How can that be? How can they be holy and a bunch of gripers at the same time?"

But that's precisely the point! Right from the beginning, God gave them a sense of place—a sense of status, if you will. He designated them holy. What an enormous privilege. And that is what God wanted them—and us—to see: that holiness is *the response to privilege, not the summons to performance.* He *calls* us holy so that we can, in yielding to him, *become* holy. Or in the words of noted scholar Dr. Gordon Fee, "We get to be what we've got to be."

God graciously gives us a sense of ultimate self-esteem so that we can live our lives from that place of significance, rather than spending our mental and emotional energy trying to find one. For God knows that such a search only keeps us bottled in our self-centeredness.

For example, if you were a general and I a lieutenant, and we happened to encounter each other on a military base, there is a certain protocol we would be expected to follow with each other based on our respective ranks. It would be considered inappropriate behavior if I as the lieutenant saluted you, and you responded, "Oh, there's no need for that; we're just buddies, after all. Let's not think too much about the stars on my shoulder. Just think of me as one of the guys." We would think that highly irregular. We expect a general to behave like a general.

In the same way, God calls us holy from the very beginning—giving us from the start that sense of privilege that comes because he has chosen us. In one sense, holiness is living out our chosenness; it is apprehending our status. Mature behavior comes not so much from our struggle to be good as it does from our exhilarating response to God's calling. God didn't just save us; he united our spirits to his and walked inside our body.

Holiness is being host to God himself. This truth is the ultimate key to the self-esteem issue. In fact, I think that the popular pursuit of building one's self-esteem is actually the counterfeit of apprehending our holiness, which is the secret to constructing a healthy self-image.

Think of the highest honors we bestow on people in our culture—the Nobel Prize, induction into the Hall of Fame, a Kennedy Center honor, an Academy Award—the list goes on and on.

None of these begins to compare with being called holy by the supreme, all-consuming, utterly fascinating, totally glorious, Creator of the whole universe! What greater source of self-esteem could we find? We who struggle incessantly to achieve a holy life can rest in the love and wisdom of a God who will work in us what he has called us. For if he calls us holy, he who knows the end from the beginning will complete the work. Indeed, we "get to be what we've got to be!"

I think God wants to so transform our thinking about holiness that when we hear the word *holy,* our first impressions won't be that of impossible standards or increased performance, but of beauty, significance, and freedom.

All praise to you, Father God,
who has summoned me to such a high calling.
You have delivered me from the struggle to "be somebody"
and have given me the ultimate place of significance;
you have chosen me as one through whom you demonstrate
your greatness. Save me from my nearsightedness,
for it is all too easy to view myself through the world's lenses
as small and unimportant. Rescue me from the world's way of

*thinking, which mercilessly prods me to assert my importance
through what I accomplish. Instead, move me to constant
rejoicing by reminding me that I've been set apart with the
ultimate destiny of letting you be you in my world.*

QUESTIONS TO PONDER:

1. Have you ever thought of yourself as "holy" before God? Why or why not?

2. What is our true source of holiness?

3. What does holiness have to do with the way we live?

4. What should our standing as holy before God do for our image of our relationship with him?

Chapter 20

THE BEARER OF
OUR BURDENS

Take my yoke upon you and learn from me,
for I am gentle and humble in heart,
and you will find rest for your souls.
For my yoke is easy and my burden is light.
MATTHEW 11:29–30

My wife, Nancy, and I were fairly young when we got married, but we thought we were the paragon of marital maturity. A few years of married life dramatically changed that perception.

Our first year was great—it seemed nothing could go wrong, whether or not she squeezed the middle of the toothpaste tube. But by the middle of the second year, little personality quirks began to surface in both of us. The more comfortable we became with each other, the quicker the guards came down, and the more the "real us" showed.

As this happened, I discovered one particular aspect of Nancy's personality that wasn't all that pleasant. In fact, it grated on me like fingernails scraping a blackboard. Of course, I look back on it now and realize how insignificant it was, but back then in the flush of young adulthood, it was a big item. And like any good husband, I took it upon myself to inform her on a regular basis that if we were going to be a couple singularly used by God, she needed to change. Not only did I maintain constant communication, but I was faithful to pray regularly over the whole thing. Such stunning spirituality!

This went on for a few months, and finally my sense of irritation became so acute that I found myself late one night pacing the downstairs family room of the little townhouse we had at the time. There I was pacing back and forth, back and forth, pleading with God. Was I praying for the salvation of the souls of men and women? Was I crying out to God for a spiritual awakening in the church? Was I being stirred with missionary passion for the nations? No—I was beseeching God to change my wife.

Well, apparently the volume of my prayers awakened Nancy, who had long since gone to bed. She came to the top of the stairs, saw me pacing back and forth, obviously upset about something, and she quite innocently asked, "Honey, what's wrong?"

It was at that precise moment that there was something resembling a minor volcanic eruption. "I'll tell you what's wrong!" I snapped at her. "You've got to change!" Whereupon I fumed and sputtered and spewed frustration, communicating in oh-so-specific terms where and how and how quickly she needed to change if we were going to continue on in any measure of spiritual blessing. It got so bad over the next few moments that I even brought God into the situation, telling Nancy how the Lord would be displeased and how she would miss out on his blessings if she didn't immediately change. Naturally, she was shocked and hurt. Yet she said nothing and quietly went back to bed.

Any wife reading this right now is probably responding in two ways: number one, you are convinced that I am a jerk and number two, you are feeling a sense of exhilaration that you did not marry somebody like me.

Well, I was soon to look back on that experience and realize what a fool I was.

It took a few months, but God arranged a series of circumstances that brought me back to that same issue, and he asked me, "What is your responsibility toward your wife?"

"Well," I said, "to do my very best to change her so she will become a woman of God."

And God, in his big Father-heart of love, in that way that pierces the heart but doesn't puncture our dignity, said, "No, that is not your responsibility. Your responsibility is to love her and allow me to do the changing."

My first response was not so much the realization that I had been a scumbag, but of intense relief.

"You mean it is not my responsibility to change her?" I asked.

"No," the Father repeated. "It is your responsibility to simply love her and accept her, and in so doing create an environment in which I can do the changing."

Suddenly I was a free man!

Looking back on that whole episode now, I not only recognize how utterly inconsequential Nancy's little personality quirk was, but how many more serious faults lie dormant in me. If anyone needed to change, it was me. Embarrassed as I was by my childishness, the whole episode underscored an important truth about living under the lordship of Jesus.

Back in Eden's garden, the sounds of joyous revelry greeted the morning sun, and steadied serenity embraced the twilight. It was a life under God's authority—a life of unshakable peace where the future was forbidden to rob the sweets of the present and where one didn't question who he was or why he was there. It was a life so secure that no thought was given to self-preservation, and one didn't have to pursue happiness, for it was in God himself. It was a life where a man could explore the treasures in another person because he already knew himself, a life rooted in God's care and provision where people were secure in God's boundless love.

And it was boundless love that shaped the ways God used his authority. Of course, God, being God, was not threatened by any other power; no usurper would or could ever claim his throne, least of all Satan and his minions. God knows everything. Nothing will take him by surprise. Fully secure in his power, he was therefore free to influence humankind through love. He didn't have to resort to shows of force to validate his authority or subdue people. His knowledge is infinite, his power unsurpassed, and his love fuses his power and knowledge in flawless wisdom.

Adam and Eve, of course, were not infinite, but finite. They did not know the end from the beginning and thus were not designed to have authority. But suddenly they snatched the role of providing for themselves, securing their future, and ensuring their own care. Without realizing what they had done, they had usurped an authority they couldn't handle and were thus forced to assume responsibilities for which they were not designed. The problem was that since they did not know the end from the beginning, they had to protect themselves from what they did not know. Since they had decided they couldn't trust God, they lost their anchor in the world. All they had left to trust in was themselves—uncertain, unknowing, and very insecure selves. Knowledge of good and evil they got in abundance, but at the awful cost of separation from the God who holds the future. Now they were on their own.

To protect themselves, they developed devices of self-preservation that have come to be known as *rights*. Example: When two people are talking, they can't read each other's minds, and they don't know what each other is thinking. So, depending on the depth of the relationship, they measure their words, guard themselves, and reveal just enough to engender empathy, but not so much that they jeopardize their own security. Postures such as these are mandatory mechanisms of defense in a selfish world. Over time these defenses become the rights by which we attempt to guarantee our satisfaction:

- the right to privacy;
- the right to happiness;
- the right to be understood;
- the right to succeed;
- the right of vindication when the victim of injustice.

And ever since the Garden, people have asserted their rights in a grim tug-of-war of selfishness that constantly rips the fabric of the relationships for which we yearn. We want meaningful relationships, but demand our rights, torn within between our needs and our fears. Yet the reason we feel compelled to assert our rights is that we have assumed a wrong kind of responsibility.

When we give our lives to Christ and come under his authority, it means that we get to go back to the Garden. No longer are we responsible for our own lives; instead, we have the joy of giving them back to God.

Now, before we go kicking our shoes off in pursuit of some spiritualized bohemian lifestyle, let's qualify the meaning here. The word *responsibility* in our culture has come to be understood as simply another word for control. In the name of responsibility, we have assumed *control* over our families, finances, and futures in inappropriate ways. The Bible gives us a word that captures the essence of the best side of responsibility—diligence, excellence, faithfulness—and it is the word *stewardship*. We are God's butlers and maids, caring for the household, but owning nothing in it. If an earthquake comes and dumps the fine china on the polished marble floor, it is not our responsibility.

I can always tell when I've taken upon myself responsibilities that are inappropriate. There are the telltale signs of fear, worry, anxiety. These inner emotions tell me I have assumed a responsibility that is not mine. Parents can, in a well-meaning way, assume a wrongful responsibility for their kids. We feel it is our responsibility to make sure our kids turn out in an acceptable way. The truth is that we as parents have one responsibility: to obey the Scriptures and apply them to our children, but leave the changing to God.

God has not so much called us to responsibility as to *response-ability*. There is one thing needful, and that is obedience. Yet there is enough Scripture to heed that if we simply obey, we will look very responsible to any outside observer. The real issue is on the inside—the freedom we discover when we have fully relinquished our lives to God's care. And relinquishing ourselves to God is not burdensome. Jesus promised that if we do so—if we take his yoke upon us—we will find the burden light.

Our responsibility is not to change our spouses, our children, our churches, or even society. We are simply to obey and let God take care of the rest. The wonder is that more will be changed that way than by a lifetime of our own efforts.

Lord God, I praise you that you have released me from taking
on inordinate responsibilities in my life.
I do find this a continuous battle, yielding things
to you and then taking them back again.
But I praise you that you are bringing me into a place of
freedom where the responsibility for every aspect of my life is
yours and not mine. One by one, now, I submit every single
facet of my life to you and release them into your wise care.
Be Lord over all, so that you might be praised through me.

QUESTIONS TO PONDER:

1. Do you tend to hold onto your burdens? Why?

2. What keeps people from allowing God to bear their burdens?

3. Why do people tend to become obsessed with standing up for their rights?

4. How do we give our burdens to God and then *let him keep them?*

Chapter 21

WHEN GOD
IS SILENT

Who among you fears the LORD…?
Let him who walks in the dark, who has no light,
trust in the name of the LORD….
ISAIAH 50:10

Nobel laureate and noted Jewish writer Isaac Bashevis Singer once said with great chutzpah, "The Almighty keeps promising things, and He doesn't keep His word."

Who among us hasn't at times wanted to point our finger at God and say, "It's unfair!"

The pathway to deeper communion with God is not always a pleasant stroll through the garden of serenity. Sometimes that path looks more like the tracks of a roller coaster, plunging precipitously into an abyss of despair at ninety miles per hour and at a ninety-degree angle. What may be thrilling at an amusement park can be devastating spiritually if you are in desperate need of an answer from God and find none.

We've all been there: contending with difficult circumstances and seeking God for answers, making not just casual inquiries, but life-and-death pleas for direction, for provision in seasons of scarcity, for understanding at critical crossroads, for insight when facing impossible circumstances, or for wisdom when grappling with unresolvable conflicts.

We cry out to God for an answer, "Oh God, give me a yes or no in this situation." Receiving nothing, we then nobly give God a little more latitude and say, "I'll tell you what, God, I don't even need a yes or no—just hearing your voice say wait is good enough." When we don't even get that, we become even more magnanimous with God and say, "I don't even have to hear your voice—just let me know you're there—somehow."

Still nothing.

At this point we get angry with God.

There are some of us who respond more positively and stand on scriptural promises that God is with us after all and that he will not remain silent and will deliver us. These are exercises of faith, a necessary regimen in developing spiritual bulk. If we're not careful, though, we may miss the reason God is silent, going on and on claiming Scriptures, but failing to understand his purposes.

There is a fine line between faith and fantasy. Faith praises the God who delivers, but it is not afraid to question his silence. Fantasy has a way of using his promises as a buffer against reality, quoting his Word while ignoring his dealings.

There are times, in the silence, when God is teaching us to walk squarely into the mountain of our impossibilities. What did he say to the mountain Zerubbabel faced? "Before Zerubbabel you will become level ground" (Zechariah 4:7). He was not to go around the mountain, attempt to tunnel underneath, nor even scale its height or soar on wings of praise over the top: he was to walk *into* that mountain—right into it, trusting all the while that the insurmountable would dissolve before his obedience.

Sometimes when faced with mountains, we are to seek wisdom. Do we go around? Do we stay put? Sometimes we are to seek power. Can we miraculously scale this height and overcome it? But sometimes we are given neither wisdom nor power—just a repetition of his command to keep on walking—right into the thing. And whether you're backed into the Red Sea or facing a midnight deadline, if God has said walk, then walk right into what seems to be impossible. How else can you prove that all things are possible to them that believe? The silence of God teaches us to walk into our mountains.

But there is another, more fundamental reason for God's silence. It can be the most revealing encounter we can have with him. It exposes things. It exposes the dividedness of our hearts. For when we seek the Lord for answers and find none, we tend to become anxious. We fret.

Silence seems to breed anxiety. Yet it is precisely these anxieties that are the answers. Why? Because they reveal the underlying issues, motivations, and fears that work spiritual death within us.

Think for a moment how you might respond to God's silence. You sought God for an answer to a particular dilemma. No answer. So, rather than walking on in peace, you begin to struggle. Something's making you—but why? Trace the anxiety to its roots—

your very struggle will reveal your answer. That's one of the reasons for God's silence. For example, you decided to buy that car or enter that merger, and now you face financial stress. You seek God for peace, but find only worry. Yet God's very silence is identifying your answer, which is found in the anxiety itself.

Ask yourself these questions: Did you seek godly counsel? Did you get specific peace from the Lord to make those decisions? If not, then you may have been presumptuous. Are you afraid of what financial collapse may mean to your reputation? Then you are too concerned about your reputation, which the Bible calls "the fear of man." Are you simply afraid of financial stress? Then your security is in things, and not in God.

Take another example. You're called on to perform some great task or take some important test. You pray for the stomach to cope, and yet worry all the more. What are the root causes of your worry? Do you fear criticism if you fail the test? Are you afraid of disappointing yourself if you don't measure up? Are you undertaking that task with the wrong motives?

Again, God's reluctance to give us quick answers is often the most important answer we can get if it does, in fact, expose some root in us that would be a continuing source of spiritual harm.

Therefore, *why would God want to give you answers when he wants to save your life?* Why would he want to merely provide for you when he wants to expose the roots of death in you? And why harangue God for answers to your problem when he's trying to cultivate in you answers that will last a lifetime?

If I worry about losing my reputation; if I worry that my goals won't be realized; if I fear criticism or disappointment—what does that say about my single focus on God? Doesn't it expose my divided heart? It is God's love that doesn't answer you because he's letting the toxins in your life bubble to the surface. As a fever is indicative of your body fighting an infection, so your struggle is the evidence that you are combating spiritual disease.

Helmut Thielicke pastored in Germany during the ravages of World War II. Like Dietrick Bonhoeffer, Thielicke was a very bright light in an extraordinarily dark time. He knew something of the silence of God in ways most of us probably never will. In discussing God's silence, he once said:

> Behind the silence—when God does not answer our prayers—are His higher thoughts. He is fitting stone to stone in His plan for the world and our lives, even though we can see only a confused and meaningless jumble of stones heaped together under a silent heaven. How many meaningless blows of fate there seems to be! Life, suffering, injustice, death, massacres, destruction, and all under a silent heaven which apparently has nothing to say. The cross was God's greatest silence...but now hear the mystery of this silence. The very hour when God answered not a word or syllable was the hour of the great turning point when the veil of the temple was rent and God's heart was laid bare with all its wounds. In His silence, He experienced the fellowship of death and depths with us. Even when we thought He did not care, or was dead, He knew all about us and behind the dark wings He did His work of love. We live in the power of this Golgotha night of silence. Where should we be without the cross?[10]

To Thielicke, it was *during* that very silence of God that love's work found its highest expression. I suggest that when we find ourselves confronting his silence, it is his love doing its work in us. When we understand this, we can then truly live in the power of that Golgotha night of silence.

Lord, again I find myself praying for a sense of divine perspective. The seasons I find you silent are perhaps the most difficult of all. I know you understand, but I am glad that you don't answer me every time I plead. Grant me the grace to receive even your silence in the face of my questions as another expression of your fathomless love.

QUESTIONS TO PONDER:

1. Why do we find silence from those we love so disconcerting?

2. Can you remember times in your life when God was silent?

3. How do you respond when you pray for answers, yet none are immediately forthcoming?

4. What can we learn from the times when God is silent?

Chapter 22

GOD: OUR GREAT CONTENTMENT

I have learned to be content whatever the circumstances.
PHILIPPIANS 4:11

*I*t is when we face our seasons of discontent that we discover what rules us. Those are the times we earnestly seek some divine provision. If our contentment is based on what God supplies, then are we not being ruled by our needs? Or perhaps we approach our problems more maturely and simply seek understanding. But again, if the only way we can be content is to get answers, then are we not being ruled by knowledge? If we go a step further and ask God for a sense of his presence in our place of need, feeling that the only way we can be content is to know he's there, then are we not being ruled by our senses?

If our peace is predicated on these things, it indicates that we submit to God because of what he does for us and what he gives to us. Yet, there comes a point where we struggle and struggle, turning this way and that, wanting answers, needing supply, yet find only silence. Why? Because when we finally stop kicking, we enter his peace.

That's the rulership God wants us to understand. Beyond his supply, beyond his anointing in our lives, beyond his guidance, beyond knowledge, beyond even the sense of his presence, there is peace—the contentment that comes from a trust in God, even when we don't sense his nearness.

Contentment based on these other things suggests a submission to God for what he does; peace, on the other hand, is the evidence that we've submitted because of who he is.

The peace that rules within cannot be cultivated when the only way we can be content is to get answers. Again, if that's the case, knowledge is ruling, not peace. The rulership of knowledge is flimsy at best because there will be points in our lives when we will just not know the answers to our "why's." Again, the silence is the answer; the struggle itself is the point of revelation. The rule of peace begins when we no longer want answers, but want only God. In the times when God is silent, we either break through to peace or succumb to bitterness.

Never get angry at the silence. Sometimes, as Frederick Buechner suggests, God does not intervene because to do so again and again and again would compromise our integrity—like parents always calling the shots for their kid, even when he's an adult. That

God doesn't always jump in reveals, says Buechner, his "passionate restraint." Sometimes, as we have seen, solutions lie in the silence itself. As has often been said, "The journey is the destination," which means that the character that is built in the process of growing is itself the most important goal.

In the same way, silence can be an answer. It is the dreadful darkness of God that Abraham knew, which is but one step away from the deep covenant of his eternal friendship—a darkness so great and a friendship so enduring that it forever renders you joyfully ready to slay your own son in a confidence that he will be raised from the jaws of death itself.

It is the prison of postponement that Joseph suffered through that shatters you to the place of utter dependence.

It is the Judean wilderness that Jesus encountered, where the only resource you have against the tempter is the Scripture you remember.

It is your Gethsemene, where your cry of "Let this cup pass from me" is met with divine silence and you are reduced to the willing submission of "Nevertheless, not my will but yours be done."

It is a death that delivers you into true life and makes you wonder how you could have been so blind as to preoccupy yourself with that which was temporal and trivial.

It is a weaning from false securities, until fellowship with God is as natural and desirable as the most delicious meal you've ever tasted or the most exhilarating vacation you've ever taken.

It is the place where you finally learn what Enoch knew: Life is walking with God; nothing else matters.

It is when fear becomes a stranger to you and pride an enemy. It is only as you tiptoe on ledges so precarious on either side—

impossible circumstances on one side and the sometimes silence of God on the other—that you learn wisdom, enjoy the miracle of divine peace, and ultimately are able to feast at a table prepared for you in the presence of enemies.

Therefore, walk into your mountain.

Delight in your struggles, for they expose your divided heart until peace rules and you are thus prepared to take up any cross and rise from any tomb.

Father, I find myself earnestly responding,
"Take me deeper in my understanding of your ways."
For to know you is to know how you work.
It is to know how you lead me.
It is to become more attuned to your
holy principles, which are my ultimate guide.
Therefore, when discontentment comes,
help me to embrace it and see what you're doing in it and
know the joy of being led from glory to glory.

QUESTIONS TO PONDER:

1. Are you, for the most part, a contented person? If not, in what areas of your life are you not content?

2. Is it possible for you to be content even in times of trouble?

3. Are you content even when God seems far away? Why or why not?

4. How do we remain content in our God even during tough times?

Chapter 23

THE REDEEMER OF OUR PAIN

For he chose us in him…
to be holy and blameless in his sight.
EPHESIANS 1:4

I once met a young lady who recounted to me a devastating childhood experience. She had been an active child, but by no means unruly. Yet for some reason one of her grade school teachers decided to make an example of her by bringing her before her entire fourth grade class and stating to the rest of the students, "Don't ever be like this girl." From that point on, she told me, her ability to learn was handicapped. Her sense of worth shattered, she turned inward and became sullen, apathetic toward studying, and careless about life. Only when she found Christ in her late teens was she able to begin the process of healing those memories.

We have all heard these kinds of stories; in fact, in one way or another we've all been through these kinds of experiences. But I would challenge us to look at these experiences not simply as wounds to be mended or memories to be healed, but as a part of the tapestry God is weaving in our lives.

Paul tells the Ephesians that God chose us to be holy. Most of us don't like the word *holy*—it confronts our basic bent toward selfishness and affronts our sense of esteem, suggesting that we are less than we should be. But actually the biblical meaning of holiness is so much richer than we think. The word does suggest a separation *from* sin and a separation *unto* God—but it also has to do with possessing an inner wholeness, where we are "in sync" with God and ourselves.

From this meaning, I suggest we could read the verse this way: *God predestines us to wholeness.* Wherever you find yourself and whatever you've been through, God's greatest purpose for you is to demonstrate wholeness right where you are. Being a whole person in this context means:

- the ability to be genuine, not having to put on facades in order to gain others' acceptance;
- the willingness to lean on others without *needing* to lean on others;
- understanding who you are;
- possessing the ability to meet disappointments with confidence;
- viewing conflicts in relationships as growth opportunities rather than as threats to your well-being.

Paul gives to us the best description of a whole person as one who is characterized by love, joy, peace, patience, kindness, goodness, faithfulness, gentleness, and self-control (Galatians 5:22–23). Deep in our heart of hearts we all want to be this way.

Yet our society places a high premium on where we're headed and what we achieve. This obsession, in turn, has molded the minds of many of us who seek to know God's best. I find scores of believers consumed with concerns about their destiny, what God's will is for their lives, and how they will make their mark. Yet it seems to me that God isn't so concerned about our *destiny* as he is our *pre-destiny.*

Your destiny may be to pioneer large enterprises, shape the lives of young children, become a dominant influence in politics, or speak prophetically to the body of Christ. But as important as finding our place is, in one sense it's no big deal. Our pre-destiny is so much greater—which is to say, *who we are* is more important to him than *what we do.*

It is often the very circumstances of deprivation or rejection that God uses to form your future. It is not that God chooses your circumstances; he is *sovereign* over your circumstances. God has allowed you to endure what you have, and his sovereignty will override the pleasures and pains that have been a part of your life. All these things work together for good in your life (Romans 8:28).

God is weaving a tapestry through the circumstances of each life and waiting for every one of us to connect to that tapestry—that is redemption. Even your past bruises, wounds, and disappointments are a key to understanding the great tapestry he is weaving for you. Our wounds and disappointments are not just memories to be healed; they can be guideposts of direction, if we let them.

People cry out to God, "Why, God, has this happened?" And God says, "See what I'm unfolding!" The tragedy for many is that they fail to discern this tapestry or, even worse, reject it.

You might say, "What I've gone through isn't fair!" Tragically, unfair and unjust things happen to innocent people every day. Is it just that a little girl is raped? Is it just that a mother loses her son in a stupid war? We shudder at the horror of such injustices, but there is a greater injustice than these.

To the civilized mind, the execution of a man known to be innocent is considered to be one of the most unjust acts. Why? Unlike rape, which is the decision of one man, or a war, which is engaged for the perceived good of the nation, execution is the considered choice of society to do away with a life. If society knows that person is innocent of all crimes and kills him anyway, we deem it extremely unjust.

The Cross was the ultimate injustice, for there an innocent Christ was crucified. The most immoral thing the planet has ever witnessed was the execution of its Creator. *But Jesus endured society's greatest injustice so that he could save the world.*

Have you ever thought that the injustices you've endured are for the same reason? We are in the business of helping to save others, and that doesn't mean just passing out gospel tracts. We are to demonstrate wholeness to others who are in circumstances similar to our own.

"You mean God put me through this to help others?" you ask. "How absurd!" Yet God has called us to be pilgrims in an alien world, who derive meaning not from any great achievement or acquiring material stability, but rather from our friendship with

God—a friendship unaffected by good circumstances or bad. As a pilgrim, you have been predestined to manifest wholeness through your life regardless of circumstances. Just as Jesus endured injustice to save others, so you, too, have been given the privilege of suffering injustice to help lead others to him by demonstrating that wholeness.

God designed us to be genuinely fulfilled as we watch our pain result in another's deliverance. Or, to put it another way, your pain can be another's promise.

I'm not saying God causes your pain; I'm saying he uses your pain. His sovereignty does not mean that he takes you *from* pain, but that he weaves a tapestry *through* your pain. In fact, God is so great, he can even use disaster to further his purposes (Isaiah 45:7).

Jesus endured the greatest injustice—but because he did, he became the supreme instrument of salvation. Likewise, to the degree that you have faced injustice, to that degree you will also be raised to rescue others.

Locked away in a disease-ridden concentration camp, witnessing human cruelty at a level few have ever known, Corrie Ten Boom could have spent the rest of her life asking, "Why, God?" And yet she allowed God to use that pain to be the platform from which she expressed a message of forgiveness to millions. The question is not, "Why, God, is this happening?" It is, how many more Corrie Ten Booms could there be if we truly understood God?

Father, I just spend a moment here waiting on you.
Show me any areas that are a source of pain to me.
Some I've already confessed and don't need to go back to; but
some I have buried deep within hidden corners of my heart.
If there are behaviors in me provoked by
these unresolved pains, gently expose them
and help me to trust the power of your redeeming love.
Help me again to see the glorious
destiny you are weaving from my pain.

QUESTIONS TO PONDER:

1. Can you think of times in your life when God redeemed your pain?

2. What does "wholeness" mean to you?

3. How does God work through that which is unfair or unjust?

4. Have you ever found yourself asking "Why, God?" over an injustice you have suffered?

Chapter 24

GOD WORKS THROUGH OUR WEAKNESS

There was given me a thorn in my flesh…but he
[the LORD] said to me, "My grace is sufficient for you,
for my power is made perfect in weakness."
2 CORINTHIANS 12:7, 9

I had no idea, when I committed in November of 1989 to participate on a missions team bound for Rumania, that I would find myself in the aftermath of a revolution. In February 1990, just weeks after the overthrow of Nicolae Ceaucescu, in city after city, from Clug to Bucharest to Timisoara, the reminders of bloodshed were everywhere. The sights and sounds of ecstatic celebration mixed with the sobs of loved ones making pilgrimage to makeshift memorials in the streets rubbed my emotions raw.

To be in a country during such an upheaval is an experience

not soon forgotten. While in Timisoara, where the whole thing began, I met a pastor who was in the middle of the turmoil during those fateful days between December 18 and 25. Hearing him recount the chain of events that kindled the revolution was both exhilarating and sobering. But what fascinated me even more were his stories of life under such an oppressive regime: the deprivation, the severe economic hardships, the unbelievably archaic medical system, and especially the harassment of the Securitate, the dreaded Rumanian secret police.

As a pastor, the Securitate became the thorn in his side, and he was roughed up more than most. He told me things got so bad that even the closest of friends sometimes turned out to be government informers. On one occasion he was betrayed by a trusted comrade and found himself cornered by a couple of menacing Securitate agents who treatened to kill him then and there. The intimidation had gone on for years. The nightmares had been many. I am sure that he begged God again and again to deliver him and his family— only to find himself frequently at death's door. But through it all he had learned something about the power of God's grace, and with an inner resilience buoyed by a faith forged in conflict, he turned to face his adversaries and triumphantly proclaimed, "You can't threaten me with heaven!" Here was a man who discovered the kind of strength found only in times of hardship; a man who discovered grace amid the thorns.

We may never go through such difficult circumstances, but we will encounter our own thorns in life. Thorns are not fun. In fact, they are downright irritating, whether they are thistles in our socks or emotional burrs in our heart that fester to the point of despair.

In 2 Corinthians Paul recalls one of his most painful memories:

a thorn that was apparently designed to keep him on the humble side. For centuries, scholars have debated as to what that thorn was. Some have said it was Paul's ex-wife. That's possible, since Paul was at one time a Pharisee, and one had to be married to be a Pharisee. Others think the thorn was a physical malady of some sort, perhaps dimness of vision or a permanent disfigurement. But I think Paul defines quite simply what that thorn was: a messenger of Satan to torment him. That's right—torment (2 Corinthians 12:7).

Trials and temptations we can understand. But torment? Many people wonder, *Can a loving God allow such a thing?* The word *torment* actually means "to beat up." You and I can squeeze the Greek any way we want, but the mental image of this word is still going to be that of the boxer being pummeled senseless in the ring. That's pretty rough stuff!

Now this may be hard for us to understand, but we're in good company because it was hard for Paul to understand, too. Three times he pleaded with God to take it away. Three times God replied, "My grace is sufficient for you"—as if Paul knew nothing of grace. I don't know if Paul got the whole message the first two times he prayed. We can only wonder. But by the third time, it sunk in: "My grace is sufficient for you, for *my power is made perfect in weakness!*"

There it was! The whole reason God allowed the thorn in the first place. It was designed to bring Paul face-to-face with a new depth of weakness so that he might be thrust to a new height of grace. God thrust him into a new place of grace so that drawing on the strength of the Holy Spirit within him would become a lifestyle, and not just an every-so-often experience.

Paul went on to say that he now delighted in insults, in persecution, in hardship. People going around making such claims are generally a few bricks shy of a full load. We have special places for people like this. Paul is either bordering on lunacy when he says this, or he has undergone a radical shift in values. Obviously, his mind has been transformed, and so he declares with the buoyancy of a wide-eyed little leaguer who's just hit his first home run, "When I am weak, then I am strong!"

The great preacher Charles Haddon Spurgeon understood this paradox. One of the weaknesses with which he struggled for much of his career was depression. But by the grace of Jesus he came to see this affliction through the eyes of Paul. "Depression comes over me whenever the Lord is preparing a larger blessing for my ministry. It has now become to me a prophet in rough clothing."[11]

A concert artist, a virtuoso guitarist blind since infancy, told his fascinated audience, "Never despise your handicaps—for they are God's way of insuring that you lean on his grace." Few of us will know the tragedy of blindness, but all of us are handicapped in one way or another:

- handicapped by memories of a childhood gone sour;
- handicapped by a social awkwardness that makes it desperately difficult for us to meet other people;
- handicapped by unjust circumstances that are forced upon us and constrict us in a dozen different ways.

Handicaps such as those can be our pathway to a higher place of grace, where we, too, can know the release of the Holy Spirit's power within us in a new dimension—a place where our weakness is but a prelude to his power.

Dear Lord, weaknesses of many different kinds so often weigh us down: our own disagreeable personality traits, unpleasant circumstances beyond our control, handicaps and maladies of all kinds that tend to so discourage us that we find ourselves losing the joy of living. But by faith I confess that you are the God who is not limited by any one of my weaknesses or handicaps. I rejoice that I am not ultimately thwarted by any weakness, for you, O God, are indeed greater than any limitation with which I might contend. I praise you that your power is made perfect in my weakness.

QUESTIONS TO PONDER:

1. What weaknesses do you recognize in yourself?

2. Can you think of ways God can work through those weaknesses?

3. Do you trust God that his grace is more than sufficient to overcome your weaknesses?

4. Can you think of examples in your life where God clearly used one of your weaknesses to bring glory to himself?

Chapter 25

BLESSINGS IN THE DARKNESS

*"Blessed are those who have
not seen and yet have believed."*
JOHN 20:29

*L*ines at the counter. Lines at the bathroom. Lines to get a ticket to get in another line. New York City, 2000? Try Moscow, 1982, at the pinnacle of Communist power. Brezhnev was still alive, and the Soviet Union was bloated with bureaucracy. And red tape meant waiting…and waiting…and more waiting.

By my ninth day in Utopia I was fed up. Standing in the middle of a busy boulevard, I slammed my overcoat on the asphalt and threw a hissy-fit in front of several astonished onlookers. The waiting game was no fun. Of course, the flight home on a comfortable jet quickly erased the memories of those miserable inconveniences. Before long, I was in the land of instant gratification, devouring microwaved pizza.

Waiting in line is one thing. Waiting for the light of understanding when we're confused or disillusioned is quite another matter. Struggling for desperately needed answers is dispiriting enough; but when, in the course of wrestling with life, we take our anxieties to the mat only to end in a no-decision, it can be utterly demoralizing. That is when we begin asking "Why?"

"*Why* has my company suffered financial reversals, when I've tried to manage with integrity?"

"*Why* has my husband stopped loving me after all the years I've faithfully loved him?"

"*Why*, after I have prayed for so long, am I not any closer to resolving this conflict?"

"*Why*, after ministering in this city for so many years, am I seeing so few spiritual breakthroughs?"

Here, the waiting game is not a matter of inconvenience, but of survival.

Faith would be such an easy enterprise if we could see what we were called to believe in. But then, of course it would not be faith. Many of us bear some resemblance to Thomas the disciple, needing to verify the certainty of a thing before we commit, hedging our bets, and holding out until the risk of belief is reduced to a comfortable margin of error.

Most times, the walk of faith is anything but comfortable. And yet the Lord Jesus says that those who don't see, but still believe have a special kind of happiness reserved just for them. When we are called upon to trust God in a dicey situation or a hopeless circumstance, it is not a matter of mere endurance, but of genuine hilarity.

This sounds nuts at first, but this is what Jesus is promising here—a heavenly take on the "ignorance is bliss" theme. The word *blessed* is a dynamic word suggesting contentment and satisfaction, the kind of happiness one wants to bottle and preserve. Jesus is saying that those who believe without needing some outward confirmation will know this kind of delight. Such a call to faith is not just to perseverance, but to joy.

Recently, during one of the darker nights of my soul, I avidly sought God for a particular answer to a specific struggle, only to come up seemingly empty. I received no answer, not even an awareness of his nearness.

It seems cruel of the Lord to sometimes keep us in darkness, but he knows there is an ecstatic happiness for those who have pressed through to faith without having seen. As I waited on the Lord, it was as though the Lord was saying to me, "I want you to enjoy the thrill of waiting, of trusting me in the dark times, so when the light does come, you will know the sublime satisfaction of having trusted me anyway."

That's not exactly the kind of response you want to hear when you're drawing blanks. Yet I knew there was a truth here, for in the moment we receive light in our darkness, knowing that we have patiently waited and joyously trusted, we know the satisfaction of a deeper level of intimacy with God than we have ever known.

It is that place of intimacy that Saint John of the Cross described: "O night, you guide me; O night, more lovely than the dawn. O night, you joined lover with loved one so the loved one is changed into the lover." It is a place that George MacDonald, one of the primary influences in C. S. Lewis's life, found as well: "I found

Him nearest when I missed Him most; I found Him in my heart, a life in frost, a light I knew not till my soul was dark."[12]

The Lord understands the emotional intensity of learning to believe even when we don't see. Have you ever considered that the Lord, when he sees us suffer, wants to rush to our side, even manifesting himself in physical form to comfort us? I assure you, in one sense he longs to. But he doesn't because that would only prolong our dependence on our senses—what we can see and touch—and addict us further to the temporal, material world. Ultimately, that would be the cruelest thing he could do, for we would not learn faith.

Faith is to the spiritual world what sight is to the material. Faith is the way we see in the spirit; it is the sensory organ of the spirit world.

God is a wise parent and knows that as we mature, we must learn to wait because of the larger issues at stake. Discerning parents know that at a given point, immediate responsiveness to their child does more harm than good. Why?

First, they know that as their child grows, he will realize that others will not be so quick to respond and that if he is accustomed to immediate responses to his slightest whims, he will then become angry or frustrated. That anger and frustration will in turn create an unsociable person. He will not know how to fit into a community or be a team player.

Studies show that children who learn to wait to fulfill their desires become more successful later on. It teaches them to be patient in line, to respond positively to another's success, to develop a much keener sense of timing, whether in asking the boss for a raise or presenting an idea, and to be aware of others and appreciate the wide variety of people's temperaments. In short, delaying gratification actually enhances the child's potential of fitting into a community. In the same way, God will delay answers in order to better fit us within his community, the church.

Second, good parents know that often other circumstances need to fall in line so that when they respond, it will be much more meaningful to the child. As a youth pastor, I had the privilege of working with my father, who pastored a large church on the West Coast. Early on, I expected Dad to invite me to preach on a Sunday. You'd think that my being his son and all would prod him to give me a chance as soon as he could. But for three years I waited, at first patiently and then with increasing frustration. I wondered, *What is the problem? Can't he trust me?* It got depressing. But I had resolved not to ask him, but instead to wait until God opened the door of opportunity. When Dad finally did ask, I gained a whole new level of confidence. I had waited and had not resorted to using the privileges of my position as a son. His invitation was not based on sentimental favoritism, but on an honest estimate of my ability, and was therefore immeasurably more meaningful. When God bids us wait, he is doing something far more precious than we can see at present.

Third, wise parents know that to reveal a thing before it can be given can set the child up for unnecessary speculation or frustration. If the pain of waiting for what you don't know is intense, imagine the pain of waiting when you *do* know.

As a kid, I used to watch *I Love Lucy* reruns, and I recall an episode in which the madcap redhead, knowing that her wedding anniversary was but days away, schemed and manipulated in all kinds of ways trying to discover her husband, Ricky's, anniversary gift. She finally found out, but as soon as she did, her face paled as a sickening sense of guilt overtook her. Hers was not the response of satisfaction but *disillusionment*—that dull ache inside that comes when we grasp something illegitimately. She became aware of the gift outside the boundaries of relationship. She got the goods, but missed the friendship.

So it is all too often in our relationship with God. In our desperation for answers, we can subtly try to manipulate God into providing them. Once Lucy discovered her gift, she had to wait much more anxiously because she knew what her present was but couldn't get at it, which in turn opened her to ugly temptations of manipulation and dishonesty. Again, so it is with God. If he is not revealing the answer to something, he is protecting you from unseen temptations, not the least of which is the bent to love God more for what he does than for who he is.

"Blessed are those who don't see, but believe" may sound like nothing more than a tricky mind game or smack of Zen double-speak. But in fact, it is a prescription for happiness. The reason that faith is so elusive to us is because we're fallen. When the Word says that without faith it is impossible to please God, the emphasis is not God's displeasure, but the simple fact that without faith we simply don't work. In other words, we can't please God because the batteries are not included.

Without faith, we can't function in the spiritual realm. Indeed, love is the greatest power, but in the absence of faith, love rusts. When God calls us to believe even in the darkness, he is keeping love alive by stretching our faith and preparing us for deeper intimacy with himself, which is the highest joy we will ever know.

*O Lord, I think the dark times of my life are the hardest.
But through them teach me all the things I need to learn.
Thank you that it is in these times that faith is built in me.
Help me to see that when you allow me to walk through the
dark times, you are in fact preparing me for greater intimacy
with yourself. Save me from "lighting my own fires"—from
striving to make things happen when plagued by great
uncertainties. Instead, aid my soul to wait for your timing in
all things and having waited, to know the happiness reserved
for those in whom faith has kindled the flames of divine love.*

QUESTIONS TO PONDER:

1. What do you think of the term "blind faith"? How is that different from true faith in God?

2. Why do you think bad things sometimes happen to those who are living righteously?

3. How do you find light in times of darkness?

4. Do you find it difficult to trust God during the worst of times? Or is that when your faith thrives most?

Chapter 26

THE MEASURE
OF HIS POWER

"This is the word of the LORD…
'Not by might nor by power, but by my Spirit,' says the LORD
Almighty…Who despises the day of small things?"
ZECHARIAH 4:6, 10

ave you ever been to one of those old-fashioned carnivals? The ones with the monstrous Ferris wheels, the sticky cotton candy, and the barkers and their coin-in-the-bottle games? The city where I grew up had such a place. Of particular fascination to me was the organ-grinder and his trained monkey. The old man would play, and the little simian, leashed to his master's wrist, would scamper about snatching pennies from the outstretched hands of mesmerized onlookers. I would just stare at the little guy, amazed that all on his own he knew how to run up to somebody and with remarkable dexterity collect his loot, tip his hat, and even bare his teeth in a wide-mouthed grin. The monkey was very well trained, and, of course, that was why everybody stood there, fascinated.

I don't know that anyone would have been impressed had the organ-grinder walked around with the little monkey in his hands, gathering the coins by manipulating its fingers like a puppet. That act would have lasted one performance, and the old organ-grinder would have been beating the streets looking for a new job. The thing that impressed was not that the organ-grinder made the monkey do his bidding, but that the monkey was doing it all on his own, obviously reflecting the patient and efficient training he had received from his master. That was the real measure of the organ-grinder's power. He worked not in spite of the monkey, but with the monkey.

I think there is a lesson here for us. Often, we think the epitome of power is a show of force that can dominate, fix the greatest mistakes, heal the deepest wounds, or rectify the most adverse situations.

As we witness thousands of people all around us daily ignoring God—when the reality of him can be readily seen in the tiniest flower or simplest creature—we wonder, "God, why don't you just write your name in the sky or part the Atlantic and prove to everybody that you are real?"

When faced with seemingly impossible circumstances, we say, "God, you are powerful enough to take care of this situation—intervene right now." Or, "Do something to show my boss that you're for real." Or, "Heal this illness right away."

But what Henri Nouwen says of Christ's ministry on earth is equally true of the way God works today: "Jesus refused to be a stunt man. He did not come to prove Himself. He did not come to walk on hot coals, swallow fire, or put His hand in the lion's mouth to demonstrate He had something to say."[13]

He can do these things and so much more. The only limit to his power is what his wisdom proscribes. But the reason God doesn't just write his name in the sky to convince unbelievers of his existence; the reason he doesn't immediately right every wrong; the reason he doesn't make you and me righteous automatons who consistently yield to his beck and call is that it *would not be the greatest display of his power.*

For, much like the organ-grinder, God's greatest display of power is in getting small creatures of dust, who live only because of the breath of God in them, to *voluntarily* do the will of their Creator.

Our requests for quick fixes are often rooted in self-serving motives, not the undiluted motivation to glorify God—for the one who truly wants to see him glorified will celebrate the hidden ways by which God persuades the human soul to do right. As we've seen before, he conquers by love; he doesn't coerce through threats or entice with bribes. The power of restraint is often greater than a show of force, and God's ability to let freedom run its course, yet still accomplish his purposes, is the evidence of his power.

Patience is, perhaps, the greatest measure of genuine power; self-control the summation of its sweetest fruits; and humility the great well from which true power springs. God will accomplish his purposes, but he will not be *driven* by his purposes. He can and does arrest the human will for the furtherance of his purposes, but let us not mistake that for desperation on God's part. He does not have to override the human will for fear that his purposes will be thwarted.

Like that of God, the true measure of our power rests in that interior place where we are no longer driven by our agendas, our needs, our hurts. The true measure of power is that we can rest in the everlasting arms—arms that do not flail throughout the universe in agitated gestures of desperation, but arms powerful enough to receive us and give us a place of eternal rest.

In the fourth chapter of Zechariah, the prophet described a vision he received. He saw two trees connected to two pipes through which oil was pouring to seven lights on top of a golden bowl perched on a seven-branched lamp stand. This was a strange sight, even to a prophet accustomed to strange sights. Not knowing what the vision meant, he inquired of the angel. The angel, surprised by Zechariah's perplexity, gave him the answer, "'Not by might nor by power, but by my Spirit,' says the LORD Almighty."

Now, that's an odd answer to a very direct question. It would be like my introducing a glass of milk to an alien who has a vague idea of what American food is like, but not a clue as to what I hold in my hand, and then triumphantly defining that glass by saying, "Don't you know what I'm holding in my hand? This is an Olympic athlete!" Of course, such a response would make no sense.

That seems to be what was happening here. Zechariah was looking at trees, pipes, and bowls, and the angel gave him a cryptic response that seemed to bear no connection to the question. But if you think about it, the angel's response makes all the sense in the world.

Back to the glass of milk. By defining it as an Olympic athlete, what am I doing? I am racing through several steps of logic and arriving at an ultimate conclusion: If a strapping ten-year-old gets enough protein over the years, he may just become a stellar athlete later on.

The angel's logic ran the same way. The vision Zechariah saw points to the ultimate conclusion of God's absolute power. There is something about this picture that gets us to this conclusion: The greatness of God's power will accomplish his purposes. In other words, this vision is a marvelous illustration of how God's power works.

Background: Zerubbabel was the leader of the first vanguard of Jews released from Babylonian captivity. They had returned to their homeland and had begun to build the temple when fierce opposition forced the work to halt. No doubt, Zerubbabel was discouraged and depressed. No doubt, he felt like a failure for allowing the project to be delayed. The point of this whole passage is that God was not frustrated by the delay, nor peeved with Zerubbabel's despondency. Rather, God was going to get the job done through Zerubbabel in spite of his weaknesses.

The Lord unequivocally states, "The hands of Zerubbabel have laid the foundation of this temple; his hands will also complete it" (Zechariah 4:9). There is no "iffy" sense to this statement—God is going to get his work done *through Zerubbabel.* Isn't it a comforting thought that our discouragements and depressions cannot keep God from getting his work done through us? That as long as we have a heart turned toward God, he will accomplish all he has designed to accomplish through us? In fact, later on when Zechariah asked specifically about the two trees, the angel said that the two trees referred to Zerubbabel and the high priest Joshua, the two graced with the oil of the Spirit's anointing to finish the work (Zechariah 4:14).

The whole passage rings with the certainty of God's sovereignty and the supremacy of his power. Yet one of the most intriguing parts of this passage is the one injunction that is given to Zerubbabel and his loyal band of followers. It is couched in a question, but is really a directive from the Lord. In verse 10, the angel asks, "Who despises the day of small things?" What the Lord is saying to Zerubbabel and everyone else is, "Don't measure things by their lack of scope or minimal size. Don't despise small things." Why this obscure command in the middle of a glowing revelation of God's power? Why would God be so concerned that we not despise that which is small?

Perhaps it is because what God does with the small thing is the true measure of the greatness of his power. Again, the magnitude of his might is most clearly demonstrated by what he does with little things—the little town of Bethlehem, an obscure manger, a small band of ordinary men. Going even further, if God's power is exhibited in what he can do with little, it is even more clearly revealed by what he can do with nothing. For out of nothing, he made the universe.

Have you ever felt small, insignificant, or even like nothing? Perhaps you are a single mom struggling to raise several kids or an inner-city pastor who has labored faithfully for years with little to show for it. Maybe you are a junior manager whose choices are continually marked by an integrity no one sees. Or you might be a singer whose songs may never be recorded, but who sings out the sweetness of praise to God with no one else to hear. These are the supreme expressions of God's power. If you've ever felt like nothing, rejoice! You are the perfect candidate through whom God can do a significant work in the world.

*I am filled with an ecstatic sense of praise for you, oh, my
great and wonderful God. As the prophet Isaiah declared,
your ways are higher than mine. Every day help me to see the
little things of my life, even the little pestering irritants, as
opportunities to allow your power to be fully demonstrated.
By faith, I would not despise what seems to be of little use or
importance either in my life or anyone else's.
Teach me the wonder of your ways—where weak is strong;
small is great; losing is finding; and dying is living.*

QUESTIONS TO PONDER:

1. What emotions come to you when you consider the idea of
   an all-powerful God? Fear? Awe?

2. What are some of the displays of his power that you have
   seen—either in the Bible or in yours or someone else's life—
   that stand out in your memory? Why?

3. What does the term "all-powerful" mean to you?

4. What does that kind of power in our heavenly Father mean
   in our lives? Is there anything we cannot do for him?

Chapter 27

HE RESTORES OUR INNOCENCE

"I know that you can do all things;
no plan of yours can be thwarted."
JOB 42:2

The dark underside of the maturing process is the tendency for disappointments to accumulate until we ultimately become cynical. I remember talking to a group of believers who were hoping to plant a church. They were filled with vision and hope. But in the course of the conversation, one individual in his early forties offered a revealing comment. "It's going to be a great church," he said, "and we're not even planning our first church split for at least a couple of years." That offhand comment exposed a cynicism bred from years of disappointments. He had obviously been wounded and was now guarding himself as best he could from further hurt. He had been around long enough to lose his innocence.

It is said that the sin of youth is compulsion; the sin of old age is complacency; and the sin of middle age is cynicism. Most of us can recall the idealism we shared in our youth. No dream was too farfetched; no barrier too formidable. We envisioned ourselves and our comrades boldly going where no generation had gone before. And though disappointments came from time to time, they never paralyzed us. We always figured we had enough time left in life to surmount any obstacle and heal any wound. We were compulsive, yes, but too young to be ultimately disillusioned.

Slowly, though, the creep of the years stole upon our dreams and mocked us for attempting big things. People didn't respond as we thought they would; events didn't turn out as we had planned; goals we once thought achievable became illusive phantoms just beyond our grasp. Hopes faded; optimism soured. "That's just the way life is," we say, as we lower our gaze and cock a crooked smile.

Of course, not every wound opens us up to cynicism and robs us of innocence. There are deep puncture wounds, like the loss of dear relationships, which simply reduce us to grief. Such was King David's wound when he lost his son Absalom.

But the wounds that leave us jaded are the scrapes of life that over time dull our sensitivities. Such things as feeling underappreciated; not being honored for a job well done; not being compensated or thanked when we feel we deserve it; being treated unfairly; feeling that we are victims of injustice; or enduring the hypocritical actions of others.

Maturing in life may leave us with a good set of street smarts, but often at the expense of our innocence. Can we ever recover lost innocence? Better yet, do we have to lose it in the first place?

If ever a man deserved to be cynical, it was Job. When we read of the trauma he endured, we marvel that he kept his sanity, let alone his integrity. But having gone through the kind of suffering few of us will ever endure, he came to this conclusion: "I know that you can do all things; no plan of yours can be thwarted" (Job 42:2). Through all of his pain, Job catches something about the character of God that, when we catch it, will become one of the greatest assurances we will ever have.

To understand this fully we need to go back a few chapters to God's response to Job's complaint. God displays all that he has done, reveals his awesome power, and challenges Job to answer him.

What's perplexing is that God spends an inordinate amount of time discussing leviathans and behemoths in intricate detail, which in our day would be like discussing whales and hippopotami. Figure that one out! Here Job has just suffered the entire collapse of his life, and God is talking about big beasts. But, of course, there is a theme running through the entirety of God's response: He is big, and he can do all things. And that's precisely what Job discovers: God is in control of everything. In other words, Job comes face-to-face with God's *sovereignty*. Therefore, he praised God not for his love or his mercy, but for his sovereignty. *The ultimate misery in the face of injustice resulted in the ultimate revelation of the sovereignty of God.*

It took great pain to bring Job to this conclusion. Though he knew God better than anyone, Job had to see that even the gravest injustices could not ultimately thwart God's ability to accomplish his purpose. In our seasons of suffering, our deepest need is not necessarily a revelation of his love, but of his sovereignty; not just that God would say, "I am here," but that he would say, "It's okay." Once we've comprehended this, our childhood sense of innocence need never again be taken hostage by injustice.

Feodor Dostoyevski was perhaps one of the brightest literary lights of the nineteenth century. Swimming upstream against the humanistic currents of his day, Dostoyevski in the later years of his life became one of the ablest defenders of the Christian faith. The man who so aptly gave voice to that faith in novels such as *The Grand Inquisitor* and *The Brothers Karamazov* was not always a man of godly convictions. In his early life he considered himself a Christian humanist, but he later adopted an atheistic worldview.

In 1849, Dostoyevski, having been imprisoned and sentenced to capital punishment, stood on the scaffold awaiting execution. During those terrible minutes, the old man in him died, and a new man was born. He received a reprieve. Yet in the penal servitude of his exile in Siberia, amidst inhuman sufferings, he discovered God once again. In his struggle with doubt, he won faith in God. His innocence was restored. He was soundly converted to Christ and could then say, "My hosanna has passed through a great furnace of doubts."

Like Dostoyevski, many of us pass through great furnaces of doubts, especially when we feel that we are the victims of injustice. But the God who restores our innocence is the God who walks us through those furnaces, and when we see his bigger plan, which will be accomplished in our lives no matter how many furnaces we walk through, we, too, will possess a "hosanna" in our hearts that the world can never take away.

*Again I pause, Lord, to allow your Holy Spirit to search my
heart. Is there any area in my life where I have allowed
cynicism to rob me of the sweet joys of your presence?
Am I jaded in any way? Have I lost the delight of dreaming?
Do I sense despondency that comes from burnout?
Lord, restore to me the joy of my salvation!
Help me to so see your incredible sovereignty that
discouragement will lose its grip on my soul.
Help me to so see your power to accomplish all that you want
to do in me that hope would never cease to well up within.*

QUESTIONS TO PONDER:

1. What factors in life can steal our innocence?

2. What does the innocence that God wants to restore look like in our lives?

3. Do you feel that some of your innocence has been stolen from you?

4. How do you allow God to restore that innocence?

Chapter 28

A GOD IN WHOM WE MAY REST

"There remains, then, a Sabbath-rest
for the people of God."
HEBREWS 4:9

*L*ife's a two-minute drill!" blared the ad. In an attempt to increase subscriptions, a prominent newspaper was playing off the feelings of frayed nerves and hectic schedules that plague so many people. The implied message, of course, was that the newspaper's information could help these people sort out their chaos and restore a modicum of sanity to their frenzied world.

Sad, isn't it? That a marketer's assessment of twenty-first-century life is reduced to the frantic pace of a do-or-die series of plays in the frenetic final moments of a football game and that such a rushed and hurried life is considered so common that it can be the centerpiece of a pricey ad campaign. To many people, life is indeed a high-speed chase for success and satisfaction, or to put it in William Faulkner's words, "the same frantic steeplechase towards nothing."

How very different is God's intention for his world! Gail McDonald, wife of noted author Gordon McDonald, writes of a Swedish pastor's wife who did an exhaustive study on the great saints of the church. Her conclusion was that the great men and women of God throughout the centuries have had one common denominator: They were marked by what she called "a holy leisure"—a sense of divinely ordered relaxation, an inner serenity that cultivates the wisdom to prioritize one's time and energy, and a productive leisure that kindles relationships and fires inspiration.

Today more and more people try to micromanage their schedules in order to find more time to get more done and become more successful so they can obtain that leisure. In fact, time for leisure has become the new idol, the new sacred rite. Ironically, when people finally get their leisure time, they are generally so tired they don't know what to do with it. This makes them more frustrated, and they end up trying to do still more.

Since time has become a more important commodity than money and even information, an exhausting state of drivenness is robbing more and more people of genuine peace and satisfying creativity. What do we as believers say to a society hell-bent on speed? There is not much we can say because we seem to be caught up in the same whirlwind.

Why is it that, for many believers, peace is the exception rather than the norm? Caught in the system of this world, our emotions seem constantly ravaged by frustration and anxiety. How far off the mark we have gone! Christ's first words to his disciples after the Resurrection were not a polite, incidental greeting. They were the declaration of the *real* new age: "Peace be unto you."

There is not a person alive who doesn't want inner peace. But peace is not something one can simply choose to have. In considering the fruits of the Spirit that Paul lists in the fifth chapter of Galatians, it's interesting that peace is the only fruit that cannot be cultivated by choice. Love is a choice; in a sense, joy is a choice, even as Paul said, "Rejoice in the Lord always. I will say it, again: Rejoice!" (Philippians 4:4). But you cannot *choose* to be at peace. Peace is a byproduct of other choices.

There is only one pathway to peace. But to discover that pathway we must first recognize something about the human dynamic.

We spend so much of our life trying to discover who we are and why we are here. In fact, many young adults take a long time to mature because of the many different roles they assume. By the time they have put on a variety of masks and experimented with various facades trying to figure out which persona solicits the greatest amount of admiration and response from other people, many are well into their thirties. This whole process delays maturity. What's left is a lot of young adults who have never grown up and who spend much of their life trying to make sense out of all those assumed roles in an effort to become "whole" people.

We usually think of "wholeness" in terms of repair—the healing of hurts or the mending of the inner self. But the idea of wholeness has more to do with having all the parts of our self working and fitting together in perfect harmony:

- our thoughts and feelings finely tuned to each other;
- our every choice informed by wisdom;
- our relationships with others enriching;
- our lives infused with purpose;
- and all things synchromeshed in an undisturbed tranquility within.

Sounds like I'm pitching a fast trip to a Tibetan monastery. How can any of us realize this quintessential bliss? Ah, but we're not supposed to—not in and of ourselves.

The only way we become whole is to get back to the way we're designed, and *we're designed to discover who we are by discovering God.* Bishop Michael Harper sounds a similar theme when he speaks of not discovering God from our experience of love, but rather discovering love from our experience of God.

Knowing God is the key to self-discovery and the fulfillment of every need. We discover God by letting him inhabit our bodies and be who he is through us. When Moses asked God what his name was, the Lord replied simply, "I Am." He did not call himself "I Do," or "I Will Become," or "I Can Be," or "I Go." He called himself "I Am."

The name "I Am" means:

- God is not driven to attain some higher goal, for he himself is the ultimate goal.
- He does not think about impressing others, for he considers the good of everyone else first.
- He does not strive to find himself, for he has always been.
- There is no need for self-discovery in God, for nothing is unknown to him.

- He doesn't have to prove himself by what he does.
- He is not anxious about the future because he sees the end from the beginning.
- There are no competing agendas within him and no struggle to find himself by trying out different personalities.

God simply is, and there is none outside of him, no power beyond him. In him, there are no surprises. Therefore, God is at rest. He is, himself, *perfect peace*. He alone has it "all together."

A. W. Tozer pointed out that there is no conflict between God's attributes within himself. His love and anger don't war within him. He is perfectly *integrated* in his being; he is whole. This is what peace is all about, and it brings us right back to the essential understanding of God as the "I Am." All of the expressions of his character are perfectly balanced and perfectly manifested. What we call peace is the perfect, balanced expression of character that flows from a perfect, secure recognition of who he is. God is not *at peace* so much as he *is peace*. There is no outside force or pressure that can upset this inner balance.

When Scripture says that God rested on the seventh day, the rest was not that of a cessation of labor, but rather a posture of being. God is still in the seventh day of rest, so to speak. The new creation is yet to come. Still, we strive to enter that rest. A paradox. But that rest is not so much the rest he *gives*, but the rest that he *lives*; not the rest he *provides*, but the rest in which he *abides*. As the one who is at rest lives in us, we shall be at peace, not reflecting the "I Do," or the "I Will Become," or the "I Can," but the "I Am."

Peace is not an absence of anxiety; it is being "in sync" with oneself. Only God is this way. Thus, inner peace is not something we attain by eliminating pressure points. Peace is allowing the "I Am" to express himself through us. In fact, we will never achieve this peace because we, unlike God, had a beginning. The need to discover is within us, and apart from God this produces an inner tension as we try to balance the various parts of our personality. The only way we can know peace is to allow the "I Am" to be the "I Am" through us.

We want God to give us peace so we can buoyantly accomplish what we want to do. But it just doesn't work that way. Peace is the overflow of seeing every day as an adventure in discovering God. Because God lives within us, we can now turn every circumstance into an opportunity for discovering how he responds.

For example, you receive a notice from the IRS inviting you to endure the thrill of an audit. You know you have done your best to prepare your recent tax returns, and as you gaze at the notice, a nauseous feeling of apprehension begins to overwhelm you. This is obviously not one of those instances conducive to your personal serenity. But it is precisely here that our true life objectives come into play. Do we view this as an inconvenience, an interruption in our lives, or do we view it as an opportunity to yield ourselves to the Holy Spirit, tossing the thing to him in prayer and thereby allow his peace to crowd out the worry?

If life is to us a series of tasks and accomplishments that we hope will validate our existence, then we will always be prone to anxiety. But if we have reoriented our thinking and have begun to see life's circumstances as opportunities to watch the Holy Spirit well up within us, giving us insight and power to respond as Jesus would to every challenge, then for us life never has to be a two-minute drill, but rather a journey of everlasting peace.

Come, Holy Spirit, and flow through me.
Rescue me from all the many things
that would drive and push me.
Center me once again in the overarching purpose
to allow you to manifest God's character through me.
Let that be my only drive, for I know that it is
only then that I will know consistent rest within.

QUESTIONS TO PONDER:

1. Have you ever found yourself caught up in the pace of the modern-day world?

2. How has that affected your relationship with God?

3. How can you find rest and wholeness in God?

4. What does "perfect peace" mean to you?

Chapter 29

JOYOUS OBEDIENCE

"My food...is to do the
will of him who sent me."
JOHN 4:34

*O*bedience is not one of the most enjoyable words in our vocabulary. The very mention of it sounds limiting, binding, an encroachment on our liberties and pursuit of happiness—not a whiff of pleasure at all. Yet the idea that obedience to God limits us, binds us, or keeps us from true happiness couldn't be more erroneous!

The Lord Jesus has quite a different perspective on obedience. In John, chapter 4, we find Jesus going against all convention of the time and chatting with a Samaritan woman with a checkered past. The disciples, if you recall, had left Jesus by Jacob's well while they

190

went into town to look for something to eat. Upon their return, they found Jesus talking to this woman. As they approached, she left her water jar and rushed back to town, telling all who would listen the account of her meeting with the Prophet. The disciples, meanwhile, clueless as to the strategic importance of this encounter, dull to any sense of spiritual significance as to what they had just seen, plodded on with their agenda and asked the Master if he wanted some food.

Jesus replied, "I have food that you don't know anything about." The disciples still didn't get it. Where could he have possibly obtained food at such an out-of-the-way place? At that point Jesus gave his disciples a definition of obedience as profound as it is simple: "My food is to do the will of him who sent me."

When you stop to think about it for a moment, that definition is amazing—for Jesus is drawing our attention to two things that obedience and food have in common. The first is that eating food is a pleasurable experience. Think for a moment of the delicacies you enjoy most, those foods most apt to excite your salivary glands. For me, it's cinnamon rolls. I love cinnamon rolls! Not so much the dime-a-dozen, store-bought variety that are stale and devoid of imagination, but the ones that are rolled with care, with plenty of brown sugar and cinnamon filling each roll in the dough with gooey delight. In my mind, that comes pretty close to paradise!

Now, there are some who have little respect for a cinnamon roll. They attack it with knife and fork like a butcher carving a slab of beef. Yet we all know that you don't treat a cinnamon roll with such mindless, uncaring indifference—you unravel a cinnamon roll, bit by precious bit. To me, unraveling a cinnamon roll is a deeply spiritual experience.

Pause for a bit of protocol. First, it is important that when you unravel part of the roll and break off a bit, you don't simply cram it in your mouth, but rather bring it ever so slowly to your mouth so that your sense of smell can get in on the action. Let your eyes momentarily feast on the sugary morsel that your taste buds are about to enjoy. Second, chew calmly and deliberately, allowing the brown sugar, icing, and cinnamon to dissolve, giving your taste buds the chance to fully experience the exquisite sensation. And third, when you get to the center of the cinnamon roll, where all the goo has collected, just sit and meditate on that for a while as you are transported to the third heaven. When I finally pop that center into my mouth, I close my eyes and thank God that he gave us the means to create the cinnamon roll.

For those of you reading this who have yet to have breakfast today, or who had breakfast and wish you'd had a cinnamon roll, can you not sense the sheer pleasure this epicurean fantasy suggests? Eating a cinnamon roll for most of us is an enjoyable experience.

That is just the point Jesus is making. When we understand obedience from God's perspective, it, too, should evoke a deep sense of inner pleasure. When we hear the word *obedience,* it should send our spiritual salivary glands into overdrive. Obedience is pleasurable because God is enjoyable.

The other point Jesus makes in drawing a relationship between food and obedience is that just as food is basic to our survival, so also is obedience. Obedience to God's commands is not optional; it is essential. In the face of acute hunger, there is no debate as to the appropriateness of food to meet that hunger. When we are ravenously hungry, we devour whatever meal is set before us. In the same way, in the face of our needs, there is no debating the necessity of obedience. For it keeps us open to the God who meets those needs.

When God asks something of us, when he *calls* us to obey him in an area that is hard for us, or when he calls us to relinquish something we hold dear, how do we respond? We usually struggle. We want to obey God, but we are afraid of or angry about what he's calling us to do. Finally, we summon our utmost sincerity and ask for his help to obey. "Lord, help me to obey you in this thing," we pray, asking for some divine impulse, some extra motivation to follow through.

Imagine yourself in these situations:

God tells you to perform an act of kindness to someone who has hurt you. A friend asks you, for example, to throw a surprise birthday party for someone who has hurt you very deeply. You feel you've been spiritual enough to have forgiven the person, and reason tells you there's no sense in getting close, as you do not want to get burned again. Or, God calls you to give the money you've been saving for your family vacation to Disneyland to a family in need. Or you find yourself seated next to a businessman on a plane who has responded rudely to the flight attendant. The Holy Spirit prods you to step into the situation with gestures of kindness and understanding, but the last thing you want to do is jump into the middle of a fight.

In such cases, we can imagine ourselves squirming under the gracious hand of God. Immobilized because God's will runs counter to our desires, yet dreading any divine displeasure, we beg God to somehow kick us through the goal posts.

God understands when we ask him for such help. And, yes, there is a sense in which we lean on his grace, not only to hear what we are to do, but for strength to follow through. But if we claim to be spiritually mature, there's also the sense that asking for God's help to obey what he has commanded reveals a sorry lack of intimacy and friendship with God.

Isn't it enough that the great Creator has spoken to us and asked us to obey him? Isn't that the only motivation we need? Sometimes, asking for his aid to help us obey reveals not a healthy dependence on his grace, but an absence of wonder at who he is.

Consider who is asking! Does our attachment to our savings account or our reluctance to bless an offender loom larger than our vision of God? We can cultivate such a rich communion with God that when he summons us to specific points of obedience we will respond with an immediate yes—simply out of awe of the one commanding.

This is not to say that God isn't gracious to impart the strength needed for obedience. But as we grow in him, we ought to find ourselves responding with quick joy because of our fascination with him and our trust in his goodness. To ask for his strength in the hard places of obedience over and over again suggests that we may not be spending enough time getting to know him.

Enlarge my understanding, Father! Give me an appetite for obedience. Help me to see daily obedience as one of the most satisfying pleasures I'll ever know. Save me from any doublemindedness; save me from secret desires that would compromise my passion to obey you. Help me to see that the real measure of love is obedience to your word.

QUESTIONS TO PONDER:

1. Why do we cringe at the word *obedience*?

2. How important in our relationship to God is obedience to him?

3. What are the benefits of obedience to God?

4. How can we make obedience to God joyful, and not burdensome?

Chapter 30

HE'S THE CENTER OF OUR LIVES

Whom have I in heaven but you?
And earth has nothing I desire besides you.
PSALM 73:25

*O*ne of my greatest discoveries came while eating a peanut butter and jelly sandwich. As there are few indulgences appropriate for the saints, I relish my peanut butter sandwiches. My other great vice is cartoons—not the Saturday morning variety with their predictable scripts and subpar animation, but the old favorites: *Bugs Bunny, Woody Woodpecker,* and, of course, the *Flintstones.* Peanut butter sandwiches together with Looney Tunes, for me, borders on this side of heaven.

One afternoon, while taking a breather from the rigors of ministry, feasting on peanut butter, and watching Fred Flintstone beat up on Barney Rubble, I suddenly became aware of God's presence in the family room. Sensing God's presence in times of prayer and worship was not unusual, but this encounter caught me quite off guard. Feeling the tug of the Spirit within, my first impulse was to quickly turn off the television, lay aside my precious peanut butter, and get on my knees. But just as I was reaching for the knob, I felt the Lord clearly say to me in that still small voice, "No, I want to watch the Flintstones with you."

I cannot quite describe the mix of bewilderment and delight that registered emotionally. The impression came so quickly that it froze me for a moment. Was I really hearing God say he enjoyed cartoons?

Of course, it only took another moment or two before the truth hit me. God was telling me he wanted to share all of life with me, even those parts I might consider mundane or even frivolous. As I reflected on this encounter, I realized that those parts of my life were as spiritual as any "religious" activity. It exposed the mindset most of us have inherited—to separate the spiritual and the non-spiritual, or, to put it another way, the sacred and the secular.

Mine was a world where spiritual things, the obvious religious duties, rarely interplayed with the more routine aspects of my life. To think of playing basketball as a spiritual activity was foreign to me. Yet what began in that family room while eating my peanut butter sandwich was a profound shift in how I perceived God in my world.

To better understand that shift, it might be enlightening to compare the Hebrew mindset with that of the Greeks. Most of the individuals God used to write what we now call the Bible were of Hebrew stock, and they tended to look at life as one integrated whole. The Greeks, on the other hand, tried to systematize life by breaking it down into various compartments that could be analyzed and organized. It made for a very fragmented way of ordering one's world. The name of the game was to break life down into various boxes of activity, prioritize them according to their importance, and deal with each according to the demands they made. So one would have his education box, his vocation box, his family box, and so on. And if he was religious, he had his God box. If he was especially devout, he would make his religion the number one priority in his life.

Now, this is primarily the mindset we've inherited in the West. We have all these different boxes—and if we happen to be believers, we have a special place in our lives where we attend to our religious duties.

We have been told that commitment means to make God number one in our lives. As a young pastor conducting new believers' classes, I would earnestly—and quite naively, I might add—reinforce this view. When young people gave their lives to Jesus, I was quick to tell them what to do next. "You used to live for yourselves," I would say, "but now God is to be number one in your life." Then I would go on to tell them that their family was number two, their commitment to church was number three, and so forth. For the high school kids in the bunch, I relegated education to about twenty-fifth on the list. Without thinking, I was reinforcing the concept of seeing God merely as a category of life, albeit the most imporant category.

The encounter in the family room between God, me, and the Flintstones jolted me to realize something about God: he doesn't want to be number one in our lives; *he wants to be the only one.* He doesn't want to be at the head of our list; he wants to be at the center of our lives around which everything else revolves. That is radical commitment.

We often think of commitment in terms of support, as in being committed to our local Kiwanis club or our favorite political candidate. True commitment to God means not that we figure out what he wants—regular church attendance, fifteen minutes of prayer a day, and 10 percent of our income—but that he becomes the very center of all we do, which makes every part of our life spiritual. Yes, playing basketball can be spiritual; enjoying friends over a huge plate of spaghetti can be wonderfully spiritual; balancing our checkbook can be intensely spiritual—as a matter of fact, it will probably drive us to our knees faster than most anything!

For Jesus, commitment to his Father was not a struggle. Their relationship was not one of several competing priorities. He did not divide his time between the sacred and the secular. He did not have to segment his life into an array of little compartments demanding his attention.

Life was not a juggling act for Jesus. Life was simple. It was a matter of one singular focus: his Father. Everything revolved around him, and because of that Jesus took hold of life with an ease of style and felicity of grace that escapes the Day-Timer set.

When we have truly committed our lives to Christ, it is far more radical than merely making God number one in our lives—a God we love and honor, but who has little to do with the everyday aspects of our lives. Rather, it is a commitment that sees him as the center and the source. It's a commitment that makes room for his presence in all that we do, in all that we say, and in all that we are. It's a commitment that can restore the simplicity and ease for which our hearts yearn.

Lord, I find myself repenting over something in which I thought I was so noble. Sometimes I really do think that I have it all together by giving you first place. But now I see that just making you first tends to make me all too comfortable with my spiritual state. Reducing you to a set of rules, however extensive and good they are, tends to ultimately anesthetize me to radical commitment. I don't want you to be just number one—I want you to be the center of my life.

So leaning on you would I be, that I would immediately fall were you to move the slightest inch.

Work this understanding in me, O God, by your grace.

QUESTIONS TO PONDER:

1. Why should we avoid seeing God as a priority, even priority number one?

2. What does it mean to make Jesus the center of your life?

3. How would making him the center affect all areas of your life?

4. How do we go about making him the center of our lives?

Chapter 31

A GOD WHO CELEBRATES

Rejoice…the Lord is near.
PHILIPPIANS 4:4–5

ecently I heard Rob Reiner, noted movie director and actor, make this statement on a popular talk show: "I can recall perhaps eighteen seconds during my entire life when I have experienced true, undiluted joy." What a sad commentary on our present culture. Here is one of the finest talents Hollywood has produced, and he can remember only eighteen seconds of joy in his entire life.

For the apostle Paul, joy was the norm. He had a concept of God that was absolutely exhilarating. He knew that the natural consequence of drawing near to God is an inner joy. Most people think that the closer they get to God, the hotter the fire, the stronger the conviction,the more uneasy they will feel. Paul is saying quite the opposite: The closer we get to God, the greater our joy. We are so bent in our thinking that we feel proximity to God is the equivalent of a joyless existence. Nothing could be further from the truth.

I was a Disney nut growing up. Maybe that has to do with living in southern California throughout my childhood, when I made three or four pilgrimages a year to the Magic Kingdom. In fact, it should be duly noted that I am one of the privileged few who were at Disneyland on opening day—at the ripe old age of six months. Of course, by the time I was five, I had quickly matured into a resident Disney expert. It was about an hour's trek from our house through the maze of L.A. freeways to Disneyland, and I soon began to identify landmarks along the way.

To this day I recall with great delight the times I would climb into my parents' car, take off for who knows where, and begin realizing halfway into the trip that we were on our way to Disneyland. At first, all the freeway signs looked the same. Then I would see the sign pointing the way to the LaBrea Tarpits, then the State College, then on to the drive-in theater with the big orange on the back of the screen. Finally I would see it—the top of the Matterhorn. With each landmark I passed, my sense of anticipation heightened until, when I knew that I knew that I knew we were on our way to Disneyland, I could hardly contain my squeals of delight. Now I have three young children who exhibit the same kind of reaction to Disneyland I did. I have trained them well.

We can all think of places or events that continuously brought us happiness as little children. Brer Rabbit in the Disney picture *Song of the South* talked about his laughing place. We all have our "laughing places"—people, memories, holidays—that we always turn to because they are predictable sources of delight.

Think of a person or situation that seems to always bring you joy. Then think about what Paul exclaims here in Philippians, chapter 4: "Rejoice in the Lord always. I will say it again: Rejoice! Let your gentleness be evident to all. The Lord is near."

Paul's call for rejoicing and his exhortation to be gentle both flow from the same recognition: that the Lord is near. Paul is not dealing here just with the coming of the Lord at the end of time; he is saying that God's closeness can be known here, now, intimately.

The amazing thing is that, to Paul, knowing the Lord was near meant it was time to celebrate. It was natural for Paul, who knew what it meant to walk with God, to recognize that the closer he got to God, the more joy he would know because he knew that the one who is the source of joy is himself pure joy.

It is a supreme irony that we, who are so addicted to the pursuit of pleasure, often ignore the ultimate source of ecstasy: God himself! C. S. Lewis summed up the sheer absurdity of our small-mindedness when he said:

> If we consider the unblushing promises of reward and the staggering nature of the rewards promised in the Gospels, it would seem that our Lord finds our desires, not too strong, but too weak. We are half-hearted creatures, fooling about with drink and sex and ambition when infinite joy is offered us, like an ignorant child who wants to go on making mud pies in a slum because he cannot imagine what is meant by the offer of a holiday at sea. We are far too easily pleased.[14]

God's joy knows no bounds. Zephaniah 3:17 says, "He will rejoice over you with singing." The word *joy* here is a pretty animated word. In the Hebrew, it literally means "to become excited to the point of dancing in a whirlwind." Most translators have chosen a less vigorous description for our English Bibles because they can't conceive of a God of such emotional intensity.

We don't trust our emotions and therefore hesitate to ascribe to God any emotional fervor that would smack of imbalance. But in thinking this way about God, we miss one of the most precious attributes of his character—that he gets so excited about you and me that he exhibits the kind of joy that can only be captured in the imagery of a whirling dance.

The Hebrews knew God not just as the God of covenant, but as the God of celebration. Again and again in the Psalms we find exhortations to rejoice. How could we be called to rejoice with such intensity except that God himself rejoices with such intensity? When Paul says in the fourteenth chapter of Romans that the kingdom of heaven is righteousness, joy, and peace in the Holy Spirit, he is describing the nature of the King of the kingdom. We have no problem seeing God as the King of righteousness and giver of peace, but he is just as much the God of joy.

Encountering the God of joy is one of the great secrets to overcoming in this life. So often the past is a painful reminder of what could have been. Certainly the Jews who returned to Jerusalem from exile in Babylon, and who could remember the glories of Solomon's temple, knew the pain of the "could-have-beens" as they looked with melancholy at the second temple. Some even wept aloud for the glories lost. But they were quickly exhorted to lift up their faces. "The joy of the Lord is your strength!" they were told (Nehemiah 8:10). To these Hebrews who were prisoners of their past, God's joy was to be their strength for the future.

For you who may think that your best days are behind you, look again. There is a God who invites you to his celebration; a God who can redeem a lifetime of missed opportunities in a day; a God of joy who will infuse you with confidence as he turns your regrets of the past into visions of the future.

Lord, again I pause to wait upon you.
Show me if I am still harboring in my mind
any regrets that are keeping me from embracing your joy.
I know that you are a God who redeems my pain, but help me
to see you also as the God who redeems my mistakes.
I bring every regret to you, one by one.
Thank you that you are, even now,
delivering me from that paralyzing sense
of regret and helping me see a joyous future.

QUESTIONS TO PONDER:

1. By and large, are you living a joy-filled life?

2. What or who is your source of joy?

3. Have you ever thought of God as a God who rejoices over you?

4. If so, how does thinking of God that way change your approach to him?

Chapter 32

GOD AT WAR— FROM A SEATED POSITION

After he had provided purification for sins,
he sat down at the right hand of the Majesty in heaven.
HEBREWS 1:3B

When it comes to the subject of spiritual warfare, there seem to be a few erroneous notions floating around these days. For some, spiritual warfare has become a coping mechanism. Stressed to the max by life's spiraling complexity, we feel a compulsion to kick somebody. What better target for our misguided anger than the devil and his strongholds—and so we fuss and fume against the ACLU. Or we try shouting the devil down in a prayer meeting, thinking that by raising the decibel level of our voice, we will somehow scare the enemy away.

No doubt, the forces of darkness are real, and we must become spiritually adept as we counter their strategies. But in doing so, let us look to the captain of our faith, who has already overcome the evil one.

When Jesus thundered into eternity with the cry, "It is finished," he announced the end of hell's dominion over the souls of men. No longer can the enemy stand and accuse those who have yielded their lives to Jesus; no longer can the enemy withstand the spiritual force of a people marked by the Lamb of God. If there were any legitimate rights that Satan once exercised over people's lives, they were abolished at his judgment on Calvary's wooden throne. Christ broke Satan's power at the Cross.

After securing the release of all who would trust his grace, the Lord Jesus sat down at the Father's right hand. *He sat down!* That is where he intercedes for us, where he is at this very moment making his enemies his footstool.

Catch the picture here. For it is not one in which a frenetic king is pacing heaven's corridors, uncertain of the outcome of the warfare being waged. It is not one in which an anxious sovereign leaps from his throne, much like a nervous fan jumping from his seat at a football game. It is one of a king who is warring from a seated position, gathering up the spoils of victory by using his feet to fashion a footstool from his foes.

Now, we are in Christ. His position is our position. Scripture tells us that we are seated with Christ in heavenly places (Ephesians 2:6). For all our emphasis on spiritual warfare today, we must remember that we, too, are to war from a seated position. We are not deciding the outcome; that's already been decided. We are not passing sentence on the forces of darkness; that's already been done. We are not even enforcing the verdict; for that's the job of the Holy Spirit. We are simply declaring what *has* been done, whether in praying for someone in need, resisting the enemy's aggression, or joyously proclaiming the gospel.

Over the years, I've led thousands of high school and college students on various outreaches around the world. On one occasion, I was coordinating a group of about two hundred young people in a witnessing campaign in downtown Washington, D.C. We had chosen a park in an area of the city that we later found out was one of the most violent in the district. So violent was this particular neighborhood that drivers could not stop their cars or drive with unlocked doors for fear that their doors would be ripped open and they'd be robbed at knifepoint.

When we arrived at the park, we were confronted with a kaleidoscope of sights and sounds—pimps, prostitutes, and pushers, streetwise waifs and world-weary panhandlers. As we fanned out through the park and surrounding neighborhoods to share Christ's love with people, we soon realized we were encountering forces of spiritual darkness beyond what we had encountered in the past. The atmosphere itself seemed to be charged with violence; some people became so belligerent they accosted us within six inches of our faces, screaming obscenities.

We knew the situation could rapidly escalate beyond our control, so we got some of the musicians together and began to play and sing praises to Jesus. Over the next several minutes we witnessed nothing short of a miraculous transformation. Suddenly a sense of peace and calm descended over the park. Where before we saw onlookers who were seething with hatred, we now saw high school students sitting down and chatting amiably with scores of men and women about their eternal destiny. Later we found out that in the ensuing hour, twelve people gave their hearts to Christ.

What had made the difference? The authority of Jesus had been established in that park through the praise and worship of his people. It wasn't a matter of shouting the devil down or beating a quick retreat to the safety of suburbia. It was the simple resting on the accomplished victory of the Christ who has sat down. We were witnessing the truth of Psalm 22:3—that the Lord lives in the praises of his people, or better paraphrased, the *Lord brings his authority to bear on situations as his people worship him.* Never had this passage been made so real to me than on that day when I witnessed a bastion of violence transformed into an oasis of peace.

That the influence of evil in our society must be aggressively resisted is not in question here. And there is no question that we should never cease to be militant in prayer. What *is* at issue here is our attitude, our inner center of gravity. We don't war from a stance of fear at the latest antichurch legislation passed on Capitol Hill; we war from a seated position certain of the outcome, sensitive to his ways of making footstools out of enemies, and at rest in our communion with God. Perhaps one of the greatest tactics of spiritual warfare, after all, is a posture of peace in a turbulent world.

It was Johann Christoph Blumhardt, a nineteenth-century German revival preacher, who actually coined the motto "Jesus is Victor," which was picked up later by Karl Barth as the trumpet call of his own theology. This was not mere sloganeering on Blumhardt's part because he was most noted for his ministry of deliverance, which entailed the exorcism of demons.

When we know that Jesus is victor and that he is seated at the right hand of the Father, we can both resist the flaming arrows of the evil one and humbly invade his domain with a calm and a security that rest firmly in the authority of Christ.

*I praise you that you dwell within me, O God.
Greater are you who, by your Spirit, lives within me than any other force in all the Universe. I would not be flippant in my dealings with the enemy, but at the same time I can rest confidently in your finished work. Therefore, I don't need to be afraid of anything that happens around me; nor be intimidated by any anti-Christian sentiment; nor become bitterly resentful toward those who express derision and hatred toward the Lord Jesus. You are in control! Help me to rest in that, aggressive in my response as you lead me to resist the enemy, but resting in the certainty of your ultimate victory.*

QUESTIONS TO PONDER:

1. What do you think are the most important aspects of spiritual warfare in the believer's life?

2. Do you trust Christ to intercede with the Father on your behalf?

3. Have you ever considered the kind of power there is in simply praising God for who he is?

4. How could we apply that to modern-day life and modern-day spiritual warfare?

Chapter 33

HIS CALL TO WORSHIP

"The true worshipers will worship the
Father in spirit and truth,
for they are the kind of worshipers the Father seeks.
God is spirit, and his worshipers
must worship in spirit and in truth."
JOHN 4:23

I have often been asked, "Why, if God is indeed a God of unselfish love, does he demand our worship?" It seems incredible to a seeker of truth that if God is a loving, giving sort of God, he would appear so egotistical as to require worship from the very creatures he designed.

Such a conception of God fosters images of a benevolent, yet whimsical monarch who couldn't get enough adulation from his legions of angels so he created humankind in order to procure an ever-expanding number of additional voices telling him how great he is. At first glance, it makes no sense.

We who have been weaned in the church's lap take it as a given that we were created to worship and that we actually find fulfillment in the worship of God. We take as gospel that God is worthy of worship and therefore ought to be adored for who he is. If I were to pose the question, "Why do we worship?" I'm sure we would all give correct answers: He is worthy to receive it; we were created to give it; the Bible says we ought to do it. None of us who know the Lord would ever question the rightness of all these responses. Still, the question can nag at us.

Let's look at this issue from a different angle—one that is consistent with Scripture, underscores God's absolute worthiness to receive worship, and yet affirms his character of unselfish love. All good things flow from the character of God himself. No debate on that point. Worship is a good thing; therefore, its expression must have its roots in God's character.

Proposition: God is love, which is not the romanticized goulash of capricious sentiment, but rather the consistent choice of being totally unselfish (1 John 4:8, 16). Therefore, his command that we worship him must flow out of his purely unselfish designs.

Love is a comprehensive concept expressed perfectly in the Trinity. The Father has always loved the Son and the Spirit; the Son has always loved the Father and the Spirit; the Spirit has always loved the Father and the Son. I suggest that part of this love is the propensity to adore one another: the Father has eternally adored the Son and the Spirit; the Son has eternally adored the Father and the Spirit; the Spirit has eternally adored the Father and the Son. Therefore, it is safe to say that *adoration* has been going on in the Godhead for all eternity.

Now, if we define worship in the broad sense of "the capacity to render adoration to another," then *worship* has always been going on in the Godhead. If worship has indeed been eternally expressed in the Godhead, this fact radically alters our understanding of his command for us to worship him.

Okay, so God is a God of love, and in the Godhead love relationship, the Father, Son, and Holy Spirit have forever expressed adoration of one another. Now, rewind to the moment of creation. At that time, God gave our first parents the greatest gift he could give, outside of the giving of his own self: He made them in *his image.* Think of that! He made them and all who have been born since with the ability to reason, to feel, to choose, to dream. God graciously gave us the gift of his image. Because of that, the capacity to worship and adore came with the package. It is not so much that God made us to worship him, as it is that he made us in his image. The need to worship simply came with the package.

Even then, of course, a loving Father-God, perfectly secure in who he is, did not greedily crave our worship. I suggest, instead, that because he is all wisdom, he looked at every conceivable alternative as an object of human worship. In less than a nanosecond, he considered all the options—the greatest animal, the most beautiful star, the most striking archangel. Finally, of course, he came to himself. Because people are made in God's image, the only appropriate object of their worship would be God himself.

Therefore, God's command that we worship him springs not from some slavish need of his to be eternally stroked, but rather from the recognition of our beauty and value. So valuable are we to him that he wants us to adore that which is of the highest worth. His command to worship him springs not from anything that would hint of ego, but rather is consistent with the nature of his unselfish love.

When I understand this, how can I not passionately worship him with every fiber of my being? Suddenly I regard the privilege of worshiping God with the most profound sense of awe and wonder.

I can no longer think of worship as religious duty.

I can no longer treat worship as an option.

I can no longer passively render worship, as I would contribute to a local charity.

No, I am suddenly transported to a place where I touch the stamp of deity within me; a place where worship is the closest in this life I come to union with my beloved; a place where I encounter my very identity; a place where I am being like my Father-God; a place where I come the closest to his character.

Should I, then, not offer the fullest expression of myself in undivided adoration of God?

Lord, in the light of the purity of your love, how can
I not but worship you with total abandon?
Enlarge my capacity to worship you!
Multiply desire for you within me until I know what it means
to walk in the continuous sense of your presence.
If it is for worshipers you seek, Father,
then may you find one in me, and may you
forever receive delight from this child of your choosing.

QUESTIONS TO PONDER:

1. Why do you think an all-knowing, all-powerful Creator would care whether or not we praised him?

2. How important a part of your relationship with God is worship? Is it vital to you?

3. Do you approach worship as a privilege? A duty? Something that has to be done?

4. What do you think are the personal spiritual benefits of worshiping God?

Chapter 34

HE'S WORTHY
OF GLORY

"I am the LORD; that is my name!
I will not give my glory to another...."
ISAIAH 42:8

Years ago, a friend of mine taught me a simple little chorus. It was a catchy tune, but too predictable and repetitious. Being something of a songwriter myself, I experimented with it and made a few significant changes in the melody line and chord structure. I then taught it to my home church, where it caught on instantly. Much of the sizzle in the song was due to my rewrite, and I have to admit I felt pretty smug about it. For a couple of years I continued to use the song at my home church and at various conferences, all the while knowing little of its origin. Anyway, I soon forgot about it.

Several years later, I began hearing my version of the song pop up in many places. It was becoming a fairly popular little chorus. By that time the writer of the song had been located and was being given credit for what he'd written. Yet I knew the song had caught on largely because of the substantial changes I had made. Of course, nobody else knew I had made those changes, and if I'd said much about it, it would have been perceived as egotistical and greedy. But deep inside, it galled me that I wasn't being given credit for my contribution to the song. And oh, how I wanted at least some of that credit! I didn't necessarily want to take anything away from the other writer; but I certainly wanted people to recognize the part I had played in the song's success.

People who persistently seek recognition for themselves— people who crave the limelight, who want to be noticed all the time, who feel the world revolves around them—leave a bad taste in our mouths. Most of us would like to pop their little helium-inflated heads and bring them down to size. There's just something obnoxious about someone who lusts for fame and glory.

When we assert that God wants all the glory in our lives, it can hit us much the same way. *Is God an egomaniac?* we wonder. This is another of those hidden questions that often bother the thinking seeker: If God is a God of unselfish love, then why does he seek glory for himself? Over and over again we are confronted in Scripture with a God who demands that all glory be directed to him. How do we reconcile the picture of a selfless Father with that of a God who actively seeks center stage? Jesus said the Father searches for worshipers. Why? Is it ego? Is it insecurity? Is it gross self-absorption?

It seems like we're trying to grasp a pretty slippery handle. On closer examination, though, I think we'll find no contradiction whatsoever between God's love and his desire to be glorified.

At creation, God breathed into the clay form he fashioned with his own hands, and man became a living soul. Every trace of life has its origin in God. He is the God of life, apart from whom there is nothing but nonexistence. If this is true, the only way life can flourish is by being connected to the source. God calls us to glorify him not because he is egocentric, but because he knows that his life is the only life there is. There is simply no life apart from God.

Iverna Tomkins, a good friend of mine and one of the best preachers I know, once said, "God looks down to see if he can find his Son in us." Now, that's either one of the most obnoxious characterizations of God conceivable, or it points us to one of the most important truths in the universe. When he looks for himself in us, or when he seeks the glory, he does so out of his deep love and desire to preserve all that he has created. For the only way we'll survive is to depend utterly upon God in every aspect of our lives.

To chide God about his desire to receive all the glory shows that we have a warped view of life. First, to accuse him of selfishness is a gross misjudgment. Second, the absurd assertion of our self-reliance—as if there were any life apart from God—is an utter delusion.

We have this crazy notion that we are somehow alive apart from God. We look at ourselves, we breathe, we eat, we walk, we talk, we even swear, then nobly relate to God as if he were simply the highest form of life—the man upstairs, the higher power, and so forth. But God isn't the highest form of life—he is the only life! Apart from him, there is no life. If we really understand that, we should want him to make us as much like himself as possible. We should strive to give him the credit and the glory in absolutely everything. It's not God's honor that's at stake; it's our survival! As Iraneus, celebrated Bishop of Lyons and one of the most influential of the church fathers, said, "The glory of God is man fully alive."

God does seek glory, but he doesn't seek it for himself. The fact that he seeks to be glorified is simply his acknowledgment that he is the only life. God cannot be anything other than who and what he is—and he is the author and finisher, the sole source of life. The more he is glorified in every situation in our lives, the more his life is present.

To the degree that I have allowed him to make me like Jesus, I am more vitally related to his life. The only other alternative is to invite death—anxiety, fear, bitterness. For, remember, death is not just the end of life—it is being in the state of nonlife.

The thing that indicates God's presence is life. Not big things, not mighty things, not powerful things. For nonlife can be powerful. Death can be big; death can be mighty. Satan, who lives in perpetual nonlife, oversees one third of the angels in existence. That is a vast kingdom indeed, but it does not define life.

God's desire to be glorified is not the clutching craving of a power-hungry deity, but rather the pure, innocent acknowledgment that he alone is life and that apart from him there is only death. If he convicts us of not glorifying him, it is because he wants us to live. If he convicts us of not yielding to his Spirit so that the fullness of Christ might be formed in us, it's because he loves us enough to want us to thrive.

I once spoke at a large conference at which I was teamed with another and better-known speaker. I preached passionately about giving God all the glory. I said that when someone else is promoted over us, we ought to rejoice, for God is glorified, and that when we do something of value and do not receive recognition, it shouldn't bother us too much because we weren't seeking recognition in the first place. Afterward, this popular communicator came up to me and said, "Well, I know that we are to give God the lion's share of the glory, but I think he doesn't mind when we want just a little bit of it for ourselves." I looked at him for a moment, thinking that he was joking with me, but he was serious. To him, I must have appeared a well-meaning zealot who needed to be brought back to earth a little bit.

The fact is, the issue is not whether or not glory can be shared. God in his love may promote us or grant us recognition, but to us it matters nothing except that it is one more fabulous expression of his love toward us. Other than that, why would I want to take any of the glory to myself? As if there were anything in me that could do any good thing independently of God; as if there were anything in me that could emotionally, spiritually, physically, or mentally sustain me.

The life comes from God, so it's natural that the glory goes to God. It's simple. But we either become careless by attempting to seek recognition for ourselves, or cruel by accusing God of posing selfish demands, when all he is doing is recognizing who he is, the sole source of life who deserves all the glory.

Father God, may the central prayer of my life be that which
Jesus prayed in John 12:28: "Father, glorify your name."
Save me from ever taking the credit, or usurping control, or

touching the glory that belongs only to you.
Let it be said of me that you received
the maximum glory for everything in my life.

QUESTIONS TO PONDER:

1. Do you ever wonder why you didn't get the glory for something you accomplished, perhaps feeling a little peeved that it didn't come your way?

2. What does it mean to you to give God glory for something? How do you go about doing that?

3. How dependent on God are you? How dependent do you think you should be?

4. What are the personal benefits of giving God glory for all you do?

HE MEETS
OUR NEEDS—
AND MORE

I want to know Christ and the power of his
resurrection and the fellowship of sharing in his sufferings....
PHILIPPIANS 3:10

When I was a young buck in pastoral work, various mentors would tell me from time to time that thirty was the age at which my ministry would really begin; that it was the age of real "anointing," when the heavens would open and angelic choruses announce that, yes, another man of power for that hour was about to emerge.

Of course, this idea was not without precedent. After all, Joseph was thirty when he became prime minister of Egypt; David was thirty when he became king. Some traditions say Ezekiel was thirty when he began to prophesy. John the Baptist was thirty when he started, and, of course, Jesus himself was thirty when he began his ministry.

That's pretty stellar company, I thought. So I relished the thought of turning thirty.

On the day of my thirtieth birthday, my wife, Nancy, and I were driving home from Los Angeles to San Jose, where we resided at the time. It was going to be a great day—the sun was shining, the traffic was sparse, and we had a great dinner planned at a posh oceanside restaurant on California's fabled coast. It was to be about a seven-hour drive, and an hour into it, my wife turned, gazed intently into my eyes, and tossed a grenade into my lap.

Do you know what I mean by a grenade? It's one of those little comments that wives enjoy throwing out for whoever may want to listen—and if you happen to be six inches within earshot, so much the better. She simply said, "Honey, I don't think you really love me." Just like that! Just a matter-of-fact statement that was as plain to her as the freeway we were driving on, but which hit me with the force of a Tomahawk missile.

"Who does she think she is?" I said to myself. "Saying something like that on my thirtieth birthday, the sacred threshold of my new anointing! How dare she question *my* love for her! Of course I love her—doesn't she know that?"

I wanted to explode right then and there, but I thought better of it. Putting on the most winsome face of paternal condescension I could muster, I said, "Whatever do you mean, dear?"

To which she replied, "Well, I just don't think you love me." Now, I knew this to be a horrific overgeneralization, a skill, I might add, at which women are superbly adept. Of course, our job as guys is to take these gross overgeneralizations, break them down into quantifiable problems we can solve, and then get them out of our hair.

So I proceeded to ask Nancy several questions.

"Is the problem that I'm not providing enough for you? Do you feel stretched financially?" I asked.

"No," she said, "I feel quite secure in that area. Got enough in the checkbook, thanks."

"Well, is it that we are not spending enough time with each other?" I knew that wives need a fair amount of their husbands' time to feel special, so I more or less threw this out as a sort of peace offering.

"No, I think we spend enough time together."

So far so good. I kept running down my list of questions, trying to identify what she was driving at. Finally I got to a point on my mental list that I was sweating a few bullets over. I glanced a little nervously at her and asked, "Well, is it that I'm not romantic enough for you?"

"Oh no, you're very romantic. There's no problem in that department."

So, with my sense of manhood intact, I proceeded to finish the list of all my questions—and I came out with flying colors! To every question I asked, she responded with a glowing affirmation of my performance as a husband.

At this point, I lost all sense of patience and blurted out, "Well then, what's the problem?"

"I don't know."

Nothing will send a husband to the moon faster than "I don't know."

"Well, if you don't tell me what the problem is, how can I fix it?" I shouted in exasperation.

"I don't know what the problem is. I just feel it."

I just feel it, she says! Well, you can imagine what the next several hours were like. My thirtieth birthday deteriorated into one of the worst days of my life. There were no brass bands from heaven, no voice from God saying, "This is my beloved servant." All I knew was that I was a jerk of a husband who didn't love his wife.

A few months later, though, it suddenly hit me. The issue Nancy was driving at was that *when she had me, she didn't really have me.* Oh, she had a part of me. But when we spent time together, she had only a part of me; the other part of me was crafting the next sermon, writing the next song, planning the next evangelistic crusade. It was all a matter of focus. And she didn't have it.

Isn't this the way it is in our relationship with the Lord sometimes? That when he has us, he doesn't really have us? The sense you get from Paul when he says "I want to know Christ" is that he wants him not for his own needs' sake, but simply for God's sake. Paul doesn't want Christ in order to be a better leader, a more effective church planter, or more highly esteemed by his peers. Paul wants none of that. He wants Christ simply because he wants Christ!

Earlier this year, Nancy and I celebrated our twenty-third wedding anniversary. One of the ways I know I am maturing in my relationship with her is that the longer we live together, the more I find myself enjoying the whole process of getting to know her as a person, without really thinking of what I might get in return.

Whether or not we realize it, we often express love for our spouse based on what we need from that relationship: the sense of personal companionship, the affirmation of our talents, physical intimacy, and so forth. An immature relationship is often based on need. We give in order to get. But as we mature, we should begin desiring to know our life partners simply for who they are.

This is the way it is in our relationship with God. The simple fascination with discovering what God is like for his sake, and not ours, suggests a growing maturity in that relationship and a growing security in his love for us. To Paul the apostle, this was the focus of life. Knowing God was not a means; it was the end. In contrast, today it seems that for many Christians knowing God is a means to something else. We often want God because we want to become whole people, better parents, successful business people, or more effective in our ministry.

Even pastors can express a desire for God more because they want to be effective in their roles or grow big churches than for their simple passion to know him. So many of us want God in terms of what we need for ourselves, and perhaps this cuts to the core of our powerlessness as believers. God is not marketable unless he is presented in such a way as to meet our needs.

This is not wrong; it's just incomplete. One of the greatest tragedies in the church today is that people are taught about God through the grid of their own needs. Unless they see the benefit for them, they're not interested.

I am not suggesting that getting to know God as the one who meets our needs is totally inappropriate. God's ultimate display of meeting us at our point of need was taking on human form through his Son, Jesus. In fact, moving people toward God by helping them see him as the one who satisfies their needs is classic evangelistic strategy: find the part of a person or even a subculture that is most receptive to God and introduce him through that doorway. But if we claim spiritual maturity, should we not be moving rather dramatically from a posture of wanting God because he meets our needs to wanting God simply because of who he is? Whether what we discover about God meets our present needs or not?

This issue lies at the root of one of the key temptations Satan used against Jesus in the wilderness. The fact that Satan felt he could trip Jesus using this tactic suggests how subtle it is and how strategic it is in the enemy's campaign. It also suggests that when the enemy uses this tactic to attack God's people, it is not conventional warfare, but a tactical nuclear assault. In the wilderness, Satan tried to get Jesus to use supernatural power to meet his personal needs. What was Christ's response? "Man does not live on bread alone, but on every word that comes from the mouth of God" (Matthew 4:4).

There is a dynamic balance here. Jesus was not denying the importance of meeting needs; he *was* affirming that personal needs are satisfied not only by God's provision for us, but also by God's revelation to us of who he is. As we walk in this balance, we are moving from being need-centered to being God-centered. That's maturity!

Perhaps this is one reason God allows us to go through wilderness experiences; perhaps this is one reason God has allowed the church in America to go through its current season of shaking. Perhaps the present problem is that we are not getting the full message, for we still, by and large, seem to want God as a need-meeter. We are still seeking God for what his hand provides and not seeking his face. Until we learn this lesson, we may continue to wander in our wilderness.

In Deuteronomy 1:26, Moses recounted the instance in which the people rebelled against God and listened to the bad report of ten spies. Specifically, Moses remembered what they had said: "You grumbled in your tents and said, 'The LORD hates us.'" The unbelief of the children of Israel was not an expression of uncertainty, but an accusation against God. God will always meet us at the point of honest timidity or even doubt. But this was not an expression of mere uncertainty—it was a finger brazenly pointed at God.

You might say, "How could they ever accuse God of hating them? After all, they had seen so many miracles and received so much provision." The problem was that all along they had seen God as the need-meeter, not their object of love. As long as they saw God as the need-meeter and not their heart's desire, they remained at a place of stunted growth. The tragic thing is that the Israelites never matured in their relationship with God. And when it came time to possess their land, they did not have the spiritual verve to go in.

In the same way, our immaturity rarely shows up until crunch time comes and God calls us to be obedient in a difficult task. Often, at that point, we see insurmountable odds; we see our giants; we enter struggles that we have never known before; and we subsequently get mad at God and say, just like the Israelites of old, "You hate us," forgetting all that he has provided before.

How do we become so forgetful of his provision? As James said, we are like the man who looks at his reflection in a mirror, but as soon as he moves away from it, forgets what he looks like (James 1:23–24). This is the great danger of getting to know God only in terms of how he meets our needs. When this is our motivation, we may not retain what we have learned about God. We run the risk of existing "hand-to-mouth" spiritually—meandering along and getting our fix of supernatural provision only when we feel desperate enough to seek him.

Addicted only to his provision, we seek his hand, not his face, and when for very wise reasons, he doesn't provide, we, like the heroin addict, become enraged. All this reflects a sorry lack of maturity. I suggest that when we get to know God for God's sake, we'll retain what we learn of God, but when we get to know God for our needs' sake, we'll forget what we learn and remain spiritually dwarfed. We'll be a user of God, not a lover of God.

Lord, I am so grateful that you know every single
one of my needs—even those I don't know I have.
And thank you that you delight in meeting those needs.
Yet, save me from seeing you only as the meeter of my needs.
Grant me a heart that strives to know you not for my sake,
but for yours. I want to know you for the joy of knowing you!

QUESTIONS TO PONDER:

1. Have you ever examined yourself and asked yourself if God truly has *all of you?* What did you find?

2. What would you do if you realized you had given less than all of yourself to God?

3. Have you ever found yourself pursuing God simply because you want your needs met?

4. Have you ever pursued God deeply just because he is God?

Chapter 36

GOD, OUR
PLEASURE

*And he predestined us to be conformed to the likeness of
his Son, that he might be the firstborn among many brothers.*
ROMANS 8:29

I was in my early twenties—newly married—and pastoring a youth group of around four hundred kids. I was by then a five-year veteran and had been driven to the brink of insanity only once. I felt myself fortunate.

We had a veritable cornucopia of programs—from inreaches to upreaches to outreaches—that kept us all frantic eight days a week. We promoted tours, built cell groups, started training schools, and launched production companies. Finally, I became crispier than a Ritz cracker and, at the tender age of twenty-three, began contemplating my retirement. I was burnt out being busy for God.

I began to ask some basic questions like, "Why am I doing this?" Yet it was just at this point of total meltdown that an encouraging revelation began to dawn in my fried little brain. It had to do with discovering God's primary purpose for me. I figured that *his purpose* should have a whole lot to do with shaping *my motives.*

All my life I had been told that God's ultimate purpose for me was to conform me to the image of his Son, according to Romans 8:29. But upon examining that Scripture more closely during this time of burnout, I came to understand that conformity to Christ was, in fact, not the ultimate purpose for my life.

This may, at first, send a shudder through our evangelical sensibilities, for many of us have made this assumption. But that's like saying we're only acceptable if we change, which, in my mind, casts a shadow over the truth of unconditional acceptance.

That conformity to Christ by the work of the Spirit is absolutely essential is not even up for debate. But it must be seen as process, not purpose. The purpose, as given in Romans 8:29, had eluded me: God has predestined us "to be conformed to the likeness of his Son, that he [Jesus] might be the firstborn among many brothers."

There it was! The process of being conformed to Christ's likeness was for an even greater purpose: that God might have a family. He wants me to be a part of his family! It's not just that he loves me because he has to, but because, as we saw earlier, he *wants* to. God doesn't love us to maintain his own moral excellence; God loves us because he loves us. He fervently desires communion with us. He wants to be one with us! That's his ultimate design. Being conformed to his likeness is the way we come into union with him, but union is the goal.

If that be so, I reasoned, then everything I do must cultivate that union. The ultimate objective of all I do is oneness with him. During a wrestling time with God as I walked through a California coastal town praying, the Lord began to run down the list of my activities.

"Why are you teaching young people?" he asked.

"Well," I said to the Lord, "because they need to be strengthened and matured in their faith."

Not a bad motive.

"Why are you so involved in developing home fellowship groups in the church?" God asked.

"Because people need to get to know each other," was my response.

Again, not a bad motive.

The Lord asked me, "Why are you so involved in evangelism?"

My answer was as forthright as the others had been: "Because unbelievers need to hear the Good News."

Now, I don't think anybody would impugn these motives. These are most noble, indeed.

Upon reflection, however, I began to realize that though these were good motives, they certainly were not the best.

What should have been the motivation for doing all these things? Wasn't it to be related to God's ultimate purpose for me—which was union with himself? If that be so, I reasoned, then *everything* I do must relate to that. Like a kid seeing fireworks for the first time, my spiritual eyes began popping at the implications. Everything I do must first and foremost be for the purpose of *giving him pleasure*. Why was I to be involved in teaching ministries? To give him pleasure. Why was I to be involved in evangelism? First of all, to give him pleasure.

I began to realize that I was a huge mixture of good motives, but was missing the very best. No wonder I was a classic case of burnout! I was not doing what I was doing simply to give him pleasure.

Since that rendezvous with early retirement, I have discovered that to the degree I do everything simply to give him pleasure, to that degree his joy and peace remain constant with in me.

Lord, the path to joy and peace is not hard to follow.
Sometimes I make the journey more complex than it needs to
be because my motivations are often mixed. Reduce me to this
one simple desire: to give you pleasure. By faith I receive the
joy and peace that the world cannot take away.

QUESTIONS TO PONDER:

1. Have you ever found yourself burning out "doing" for God? What did you do about it?

2. What do you believe is the ultimate scriptural purpose for your life?

3. How important is conformity to the image of Christ to you?

4. What does union with God mean to you? How can you cultivate that?

Chapter 37

HE POURS OUT
HIS MERCY

The steadfast love of the LORD never ceases,
his mercies never come to an end;
they are new every morning; great is your faithfulness.
LAMENTATIONS 3:22–23, NRSV

My Uncle Curly was a redneck's redneck. Raised in the deep South, he was a good ol' boy for whom a good time was shootin' raccoons. I never got that close to him—nobody could, really. You see, my uncle was one of the most ornery men you could possibly meet. He despised African-Americans. He was the sort of bigot that made Archie Bunker look like a Harvard liberal.

When my Aunt Billie and Curly married, they were not believers. A few years after their marriage, however, my aunt was radically converted to Christ. However, Curly would have nothing to do with her newfound religion. In fact, he soon came to loathe her faith and regularly berated her for her pursuit of God.

My aunt persevered and became quite an illuminating Bible teacher. Over the years, as her teaching ministry grew, she became more and more in demand as a speaker. To my Uncle Curly, this meant absolutely nothing. In fact, the more "religious" she got, the more obnoxious he became. Friends of hers who would brave a phone call to her house would often hear Curly's surly voice on the other end cursing and swearing at them. I don't think I ever saw the old crank smile.

When one of Curly's daughters married an African-American, you can imagine how such a man, blinded by prejudice, reacted. It enraged him when their first daughter was born! This was *his* granddaughter, a child of *his* bloodline mixed with the blood of a black man. Curly was so incensed that he refused to ever see her.

Year after year went by. Now into his seventies, emaciated by emphysema—the grim evidence of the three-pack-a-day habit he indulged throughout most of his life—he became even more mean-spirited. Shutting himself away in his little room with his little TV, he locked the rest of the world out, wasting his sorry days in isolated misery. For thirty years my aunt, and so many others, had diligently prayed for his salvation, yet he never registered a flicker of interest. He just grew more sullen and hateful.

He faced death's door I don't know how many times, and each time he faced it, he belligerently refused to hear anything about God's love for him. We knew his days were numbered, but all of us, except perhaps my aunt, had completely given up hope that he would ever come to the Lord. After thirty years of prayer and countless opportunities for him to receive Christ personally, we figured that he was probably the kind of person Paul talks about in the first chapter of Romans: the reprobate individual completely given over to a debauched mind, for whom there was now no more chance to be saved. We just assumed he was too far gone.

A few months before he died, that little granddaughter, now four years of age—the offspring of the mixed marriage he so despised—came into the room where he lay dying. Too weak to curse at her, he lay there as she tiptoed into the room.

"Papa," she said, "you need to give your heart to Jesus because I may never be able to tell you about his love again."

Upon hearing those words, his eyes suddenly glistened with tears. This friendless man who was riddled with hate, who had wasted his entire life; this obnoxious coot, who by the uncaring indifference that had shaped his miserable soul had been the source of grief to so many for so long—this man heard the voice of the granddaughter he had so rejected plead with him.

"You need to pray and ask Jesus into your heart."

In a flash, she was gone. But something happened in that room over the next few minutes. A hardened heart, hardened for who knows how long, quickly melted. That precious little object of his derision became the source of his salvation. Suddenly God touched him, and he committed his life right then and there to the Lord Jesus Christ.

It was genuine, too. In the remaining months of his life, feeble as he was, he made sure that he called every one of his relatives and told them of what he had done and of their absolute need to make their hearts right with God. He spent his final few months sharing God's love with his family, the medical staff that attended him, and anybody else who would listen. The man had been completely changed.

When I heard of his changed life and of his newfound relationship with Jesus, I, like so many who knew him, was absolutely stunned. For I had never known a person for whom change seemed so utterly impossible. He was the hardest case I had ever seen, yet he was not too hard a case for the love of Jesus.

I encountered the mercy of God in a new way the day I heard of his conversion. I realized how big and how vast and how mighty must be God's mercy to melt such a hardened man.

I, of course, am not such a tough case. I'm not as stubborn as the next guy. I'm a decent citizen, not a hardened criminal. I'm not as needy of mercy as the lifer doing time in the state pen. I know I need grace. But mercy's for the bad guys who plead for it. I'm not so bad—at least *I* don't think so.

The Scriptures say that God's mercies are new every morning. This can strike us in one of two ways. To those of us who sense the extremity of our need, it comes as the overwhelming relief of a last-minute stay of execution. To those of us who feel that we are not too bad after all, it seems a bit puzzling. We usually sense our need of mercy only when, by our own measurement, we've messed up pretty good. Otherwise, our self-images are sound, and we think we're fairly likable people.

Yet have we ever thought that the fresh overtures of God's mercies suggest our constant sense of need? Maybe we really don't see what we'd be like apart from God's grace. Am I convinced that I need his mercies every morning? Not just some mornings, not just the mornings I'm desperate, but every morning?

Have I been radically challenged by my sense of ineptness and my need to depend on him?

Have I been convinced that apart from him no good thing dwells in me?

Have I been radically convinced that even my choices to worship and obey him spring from the influencing power of the Holy Spirit within me?

Unless I'm allowing the Holy Spirit to constantly reveal to me what I am apart from his work of grace, I will not understand why it is so necessary for God's mercies to be made new *for me* every morning, whether or not I sense I need it. Perhaps my greatest need is to be shown my need and to ask God daily to reveal to me where and why I need his mercies *this* day. Maybe then humility will not be so much a matter of constantly trying to rein in an errant ego as it will be the natural response to my desperate need for his mercy. It is my understanding of why I continuously need his mercy that cleanses me of my stench of self-righteousness.

I praise you, O God, that you don't give me what I deserve. When I contemplate your mercies, my gratitude knows no bounds. Thank you that the expression of your mercy is not the sporadic gestures of a capricious God, but the generous displays of your desire for me. I don't shrink from seeing the enormity of my weakness, nor do I shrink from conviction of sin. For through it all I know that in opening my heart to your dealings, I will ultimately feast on your mercies.

QUESTIONS TO PONDER:

1. Why do you think showing mercy is so hard?

2. What does it mean to you that God's mercies are new every day?

3. If we are bitter or resentful towards someone, what steps can we take to soften our hearts toward him or her?

4. Can you think of three instances in Scripture where God showed mercy to a person or a nation who had committed reprehensible acts? What do you think the psalmist meant when he wrote, "His mercies endure forever"?

Chapter 38

A GOD WHO SATISFIES THE MIND

Since the creation of the world God's invisible qualities—
his eternal power and divine nature—have been clearly seen.
ROMANS 1:20

hen my son Cameron was ten years old, he came to me
one day, bothered by God's invisibility. "Why can't we see God?" he
asked. "I think if I could see him, it would make it easier for me to
believe."

These are the times when parents hastily send prayers of desperation up to heaven. "Help me think fast on my feet on this one,
God!" we pray. Of course, when your kids pose the tough questions, the safest play is to hit the ball back into their court.

"Why do you think God is invisible?" I asked him.

"Well—" he thought for a moment—"probably because, number one, he's already tried being visible, and it didn't seem to work for a lot of people. And number two, if he were visible, for all of us to see at the same time, we'd end up with a bunch of little gods around the world, and he wouldn't be the one big, powerful God he is. 'Cause I guess the only way he can be everywhere to all people is to be invisible."

Now that's a pretty astute response. Cameron saw that God has already revealed himself in human form in Christ Jesus, demonstrating the fullness of his power and love, and that most people still did not believe in him even while he ministered in Palestine. And God knows the hearts of men and women; they are the same in every generation. If Christ were to come to each society throughout the earth in every generation, the response would be the same—most would not believe, and those who did wouldn't need physical proofs. Second, Cameron connected the power of God's omnipresence with the necessity of his invisibility to the naked eye.

We all confront mental barriers such as these in the course of our journey. Sometimes unresolved questions that assault our intellect can become unresolved hurts. Unresolved questions such as:

- If God is a God of love, why is there war?
- Why is Jesus "the only way" to have a relationship with God?
- How do we make sense of God as a trinity of persons—one in three, three in one?

A lot of people just throw their hands up in desperation and futility when it comes to understanding God. "Just too mysterious for me," they often say. There are some whose hearts never warm toward God because they have these questions and feel they have to shift their minds into neutral in order to find a relationship with the divine. And for those of us who look for reasons to believe, blind leaps of faith become very risky propositions.

Let's take this issue of God as Trinity. I recall years ago reading of one superstar athlete who grew up in a Christian environment, but as an adult converted to Islam. He was asked why he made the switch, and his response was that Christianity was just too confusing, with too many doctrines like the Trinity. So he opted out in the name of confusion—it was all just too perplexing for him, and he wanted something he thought was much simpler and tidier.

Yet, is it really all that hard to understand this concept of God as the Father, Son, and Holy Spirit? If we stop and think carefully, I believe we'll find that the idea of the Trinity is the highest possible conception of the nature of God and that it needn't be a stumbling block anymore.

Most of us cozy to the idea that God is a God of love. If God exists, we trust—based on the goodness we sense around us—that he is a loving God. To my mind, this presents one of the most potent arguments in favor of God as Trinity. Consider: How do we know that love exists? For love to be verified, there has to be an object of its energies. If there's nothing to love, then you never know whether or not love exists.

Take, for example, a Muslim's conception of God. When there was no one in existence but Allah, who is perceived as a singular personality, how do you know whether or not he was love? You don't. You can put your trust in the teachings of the Koran and hope that what you believe is right, but there is nothing inherent in his nature that verifies the presence of love.

On the other hand, I believe that God as Trinity—God as plurality—substantiates the eternity of love, for there has always been an object of affection within the Godhead. We can speak of three distinct personalities, abiding in such a comprehensive unity that we are at the same time speaking of one God manifested in three persons.

Why does this substantiate love? Because the Father has always had an object of love—he's always loved the Son and the Spirit; the Son has always loved the Father and the Spirit; the Spirit has always loved the Father and the Son. In other words, love has always existed within the Godhead.

To my mind, this revelation of God is vastly superior to the idea of God existing as singular in nature. We not only have the written record of his words in Scripture, but his very nature offers us the proof that love is an eternal reality. No wonder, then, that the poet John Donne prayed with such affectionate fervor, "Batter my heart, Three-Personed God!"

This doesn't fully solve the mystery. Nor should it. C. S. Lewis says, "One reason I believe in the Trinity is that no human could have thought it up."[15] There is always a healthy sense of "the other" about God, and if we lose that, we can be brought perilously close to the dangers of conceiving God in our image. Nonetheless, God has so disclosed himself to us that we can know the wisdom behind the mystery. It just makes sense that God is a plurality of persons who have existed throughout eternity as one.

Of course, God isn't on trial and never plays the patsy to skeptics. But intellectual hurdles such as the Trinity of God keep many from knowing his love. In the extravagance of his grace, God reveals himself, showing us that there are wise and loving reasons why he is the way he is. As we discover them, we will celebrate his wonder.

Thank you, God, that you are not afraid of my
questions, nor are you displeased with my doubts.
Lord, I bring to you now all of my unresolved questions.
Thank you that you don't quickly answer every one of
them, for it means that you are affording me the
delight of spending time seeking you,
which will only bond me more strongly to you.
For I know, as you said to the prophet Jeremiah,
that you will be found if we seek you with all our hearts.

QUESTIONS TO PONDER:

1. How do you respond to the really tough questions about the person of God?

2. How well do you understand the Trinity? What does that mean to you as far as your relationship with God is concerned?

3. How do you deal with your own tough inner questions and doubts about God, his Word, and who he is?

4. Why do you think God has left us with these kinds of mysteries concerning himself?

Chapter 39

GOD'S CALL TO DEPENDENCE

"Apart from me you can do nothing."
JOHN 15:5B

ecently I found myself on a plane talking with a rather well-to-do woman who handled pension plans for multinational companies. She was quite well connected and widely traveled. But as we began talking about spiritual things, she soon divulged her interest in the paranormal, including the fact that she had had several of what she considered out-of-body experiences.

We got to talking about depending on God, and this took us to a familiar argument that many people use against God. It is the argument that says, "You Christians just use God as a crutch."

I told this woman, "Of course God is a crutch! He is the ultimate crutch! I have no problem, nor am I embarrassed, in admitting that. I am absolutely dependent upon God, who is the source of all life and being."

You see, this argument goes to the root of what is wrong with the human race. The feminists protest this, the left-wingers protest that, the gun lobby protests something else; and though many protesters have legitimate complaints, most of their rhetoric is a demand for rights. And then we wonder why it's hard to arrive at some place of unity. It's because a bunch of *self-reliant* people can't get along.

We have to learn radical dependence first. And the only person worthy of our dependence is God. I suggest that if everybody understood just how much he or she needed that "crutch," the world would be a better place. But since Adam and Eve took that infamous bite of the forbidden fruit, people have incessantly attempted to make it on their own, treating as infantile the notion that we are utterly dependent on God.

In the Garden, it was Adam who sealed the fate of mankind. For even though Eve had already partaken of the fruit, Adam could have saved the human race from its present condition. We don't know what would have happened to Eve, but Adam would have survived and perhaps God would have made him another partner. But the tragedy of Adam is that when he saw his wife eat the fruit and not die, he trusted his senses and his interpretation of the facts far more than he trusted the word of the Lord. Discarding the "crutch," he assessed the matter on his own and decided to take the course of action he thought best: He ate the fruit.

The way we view this dependence question has a measurable

bearing on our perception of God's power. And it also explains why God allows the seemingly impossible to continually confront us.

God is in the business of magnifying himself in our eyes. This is not an ego trip on his part. Quite the contrary: It's meant to ensure our security. He exposes us to a myriad of circumstances that provoke fear or anxiety only so that he can reveal himself as more than able to meet those fears and match those anxieties. He wants to take us to dead ends in our lives so that he can show us he's greater than the dead end. He wants to take us to the Red Seas of our lives so that he can show us that he's greater than Pharaoh's army.

You may recall that the route the Israelites took to the Red Sea was a long way from the route they could have taken into Sinai's desert. But God purposely led them out of the way to the impossible place so that he could reveal himself as more potent than the might of Egypt.

So when you think that God is taking too much time to get you where you need to be, or when you think you have been backed against the Red Sea and face the hot breath of the enemy, be reassured that God has positioned you for a revelation of his power.

The whole idea of self-reliance is questionable at best. We have this view of ourselves as fundamentally self-directed, autonomous beings in whom maturity is best evidenced by how independent we become. We play God in our own lives, easily forgetting what H. G. Wells once observed—that as soon as man thinks he is God, he begins to act like the devil.

The idea of being dependent on anything or anybody smacks of weakness to us. But the nature of God in his Trinity suggests that singularity is actually illusory. If God himself is three persons—Father, Son, and Holy Spirit—in a comprehensive, perfectly unified plurality, then where do I get off thinking that I am singularly complete in and of myself?

Quite the contrary, God has wonderfully designed me as fundamentally incomplete—designed to find my completeness as I rightly relate to God and to others. Dependence is not weakness; it is owning up to the reality of things. It is an absolute reliance on God based not on our need alone, but on God's design in demonstrating his glorious power.

Such a "dependent personality" does not produce a social parasite, sucking the life out of any and all; it produces a person refreshingly freed from a preoccupation with himself. Oswald Chambers thus exhorts us, "Let the attitude of your life be a continual dependence upon God, and your life will have an ineffable charm about it."[16]

Years ago, the eminent French philosopher Jean-Paul Sartre wrote *No Exit,* a play that captured for a generation the sense of entrapment in a miserable, senseless world in which there is little hope. But it is precisely when we feel there is "no exit," precisely at the points we are confronted with our limitations and impossibilities, that we grasp the revelation of God's power.

God cannot show himself powerful to those who feel adequate and whose confidence is in their own abilities. People often say it's only when we hit periods of weakness that we become tender toward the things of the Lord. That's nonsense. It has nothing to do with our weakness; it has everything to do with God purposely bringing us to that place of weakness so that he can manifest his power to us.

God is not just getting us to the place where we can depend on the divine crutch, though that is what we need to do. Rather, he's allowing us a glimpse of his power at the point of our impossibilities so that we might know the joy of being effective in his purposes. Your pain is a potential power encounter with God. In all, let's never forget that whatever we do without God, we must, in the words of George MacDonald, "fail miserably—or succeed more miserably."[17]

Once again, I am filled with a sense of praise and gratitude
that you have not left me alone to navigate in this world.
Thank you that you are not some sort of divine watchmaker
who simply wound me up to observe me from a distance.
No, you are intimately involved with every facet of my life,
and you call me to depend on you utterly in the tiniest detail.
I know that as I yield to you, this kind of yieldedness will
allow you to work in me the character and nature of your
Son, Jesus, and I know that his kind of life
is the most fulfilling that can ever be known.

QUESTIONS TO PONDER:

1. Have you ever heard someone say in a critical way that God is nothing more than "a crutch"?

2. How dependent are you on God, even during times when you feel things are not going well?

3. Do you ever find yourself drifting from God—even a little—when your life is "in order"?

4. Do you ever feel inadequate, only to have God pick you up and show you that your adequacy is in him?

Chapter 40

FACE-TO-FACE WITH GOD

I saw the Lord seated on a throne, high and exalted,
and the train of his robe filled the temple.
Above him were seraphs…and they were calling to one another:
"Holy, holy, holy is the LORD Almighty;
the whole earth is full of his glory."
ISAIAH 6:1–3

It was one of those searing hot days the Middle East is known for. On the arid hillside of the Mount of Olives, overlooking the hallowed eastern gate of Jerusalem, hundreds of intercessors had gathered. Scripture says it is this mount that the feet of Christ will touch first when he returns to earth. Envisioning what it will be like on that day the King of kings marches through the eastern gate, unfurling his authority to the world, transfixed us all in the grip of eternal destiny. For five afternoons we knelt on that dry, dusty slope, ardently praying for the nations.

On the last day of the event, a large company of celebrants, dancing and carrying colorful banners, proceeded down the Mount of Olives to the stirring strains of two of my choruses, penned to capture a sense of the Lord's majesty and ultimate triumph:

The kingdoms of this world
Have become the Kingdoms of our God
And of His Christ forever,
And He shall reign forever and ever.
Lift up your heads to your coming King:
Bow before Him and adore Him, sing
To His majesty, let your praises be
Pure and holy, giving glory to the King of kings.

Chills ran down my spine as I watched this great company of dancers and singers and banner-carriers shouting, singing, and extolling the glories of God. It was an electric spectacle that, for me, foreshadowed that great day when every knee shall bow and every tongue confess that *Jesus Christ is Lord*—to the praise of God the Father.

In that same moment I touched a little of the wonder that must have struck the prophet Isaiah when a vision of God's glory captivated him. Scripture says that in the year King Uzziah died, Isaiah lifted up his eyes to the heavens and was whisked away in spirit to the antechambers of God's holy sanctuary (Isaiah 6). You may recall that Uzziah was something of a national hero, who had restored the nation's former splendor after a long period of decline. Uzziah was a godly man, too, a king who had brought stability, morality, security, peace, and comfort to his people. How Isaiah must have admired him—and how he must have been smitten with grief at Uzziah's sudden passing.

Yes, when Uzziah died, all that was secure for Isaiah must have died along with the great man who was his king, mentor, and hero. No doubt Isaiah felt bereft and shaken, as if an earthquake had rocked the foundations of life. How could he have known that this shaking was but the preparation for something greater to take place—the prelude of new vision, spiritual strength, and maturity? How could he have known that out of loss and insecurity would come power, direction, and a call to the life's mission God had for him?

As Isaiah went on after Uzziah's death, he must have felt only confusion. And then—Isaiah lifted his eyes above his circumstances. And that was when he was caught up in a vision of glory—the glory of God that continually shines above this earthly plain, whether or not our eyes are open to see it.

Transported into realms of heavenly wonder, Isaiah must have been startled by the unspeakable beauty of the heavenly temple that appeared before him. What bright majesty did he see? What kind of purity? Isaiah recorded few details for us, so great was his awe.

But we can imagine him inching along the corridors of the heavenly sanctuary. What was this throng of bright beings he found himself moving among? It was the host of heaven! The retinue of angelic worshipers, filling the place shoulder to shoulder, crowded together to catch a glimpse.

But a glimpse of what?

Isaiah must have pressed forward, only to be shattered by the sight that greeted his eyes: above a great throne, angels on-the-wing. The great seraphs, blazing with a singular fiery passion, their eyes fixed on one thing alone—the one whose lovely, terrible beauty spilled from the throne. The one for whom all creation waits. The center of the very universe. Unable to take their eyes from him, the angels cried, *"Holy, holy holy…."*

But Isaiah's still-mortal eyes could not look upon him. All in a moment, he was taken by the joy, the wonder, the longing—and the fear that he had looked upon purity itself. "Woe is me, I am ruined!" Isaiah cried.

Does Isaiah's response seem as odd to you as it does to me? Why didn't he shout with the angels, "Holy is the Lord"?

One possibility occurs to me: In the moment when Isaiah was consumed by morbid thoughts of his own pain and loss and need, he was transported into the presence of the all-in-all, the one who is the selfless outpouring of holiness, love, goodness, compassion, guidance, provision—everything that our souls need in order to live.

I wonder if Isaiah saw himself for what he was: a self-centered being, a man who had found his security, stature, and well-being in an earthly relationship with a mortal man who, though a king, was doomed to die.

Did Isaiah really see his own littleness? Did he see his misplaced dependence on a man? Perhaps. We do know that he saw into the burning depths of God and cried, "Woe is me…."

I do know that I am a lot like Isaiah when I mistakenly look for my security and the fulfillment of life's needs in anything this life offers. We love. We work. We plan. We build homes and dreams. And, of course, we should never be so otherworldly that we refuse to see the goodness and blessing of God in created things.

But I also know that God must do for me what he did for Isaiah. And that is to shake, or even remove, the very things on which I stake my security and well-being. It seems he must remove the Uzziahs from my life in order to lift my vision above this earthly plain and my own pain of loss so that he can show *himself*.

What else can pull us out of our imprisoning self-centeredness but a true vision of God, the selfless one? As A. W. Tozer has so astutely stated, "To regain her lost power the Church must see heaven opened and have a transforming vision of God."[18]

We will have many losses, hurts, and needs in this life. That is the nature of our life here beneath heaven. But the healing of our souls—the feeding, growth, and maturity of our inner man—will not come as we focus on our needs. It will never come if we stare intently into the emptiness and longing that is in us. All we will see is ourselves, and that is the sure road to grief, cynicism, boredom, or despair.

Our greatest need is to abandon ourselves in worship—to cry out for a new glimpse of the one our souls long for: the God who heals our hurts, fills our needs, and directs our steps with his appearing. For in his marvelous, many-faceted self lie the answers and comforts to all our needs.

Isaiah needed a face-to-face encounter with God. After it, he was no longer absorbed in himself; he was renewed from within by the dazzling wonder of God. His life was transformed. Like a laser, it was focused on one burning passion: to make this wonderful God known to the ends of the earth. Out of great loss Isaiah lifted his eyes, saw God, and so began the true mission for which he had been created.

That is how it is for you and me as well. God may need to put his finger on the earthly thing on which we have fixed our sense of purpose and well-being. And when the shaking is done and we are standing alone in our fear, we have the chance to lift our eyes and see the glory of the Lord, if we will surrender totally to him.

Dear Father-God of all wonders, heal my hurt, fill my need, direct my steps through visions of you. Teach me to know you, and make me ready to serve others for whom your heart is aching. Yes, make me a vessel shaped by you, containing only the truth about your excellent virtues that fill the whole earth and heaven, too. Heal my soul, Father, and make me ready to answer your call, so that, like Isaiah, when you need an obedient child to serve you here on earth, I will hear your call and say, "Here am I—send me!"

QUESTIONS TO PONDER:

1. How would you describe "God's glory"?

2. Contrast that with your own human imperfection. How do you see yourself relating to God in light of that?

3. Has God ever shaken you to the point where you realized your security was totally in him?

4. Do you ever appreciate the goodness of God when you look at created things?

NOTES

1. C.S. Lewis, *An Anthology of C.S. Lewis*, ed. Clyde S. Kilby (New York: Harcourt, Brace & World, 1969), 22, 24.

2. Oswald Chambers, *My Utmost for His Highest* (New York: Dodd Mead & Company, 1935), 31.

3. J. George Mantel, *Beyond Humiliation* (Minneapolis, Minn.: Dimension Books, Bethany Fellowship, Inc., 1975), 35.

4. A. W. Tozer, *The Knowledge of the Holy* (New York: Harper & Row Publishers, 1961), 113.

5. Michael Quoist, *Prayers of Life* (London: Gile Publishers, 1963), 102.

6. Donald Bloesch, *Essentials of Evangelical Theology*, vol. 1 (New York: Harper & Row Publishers, 1978), 41.

7. Francis Thompson, *Selected Poems of Francis Thompson* (London: Methuen and Co., 1909), 55-6.

8. Chambers, *My Utmost for His Highest*, 154.

9. Jonathan Edwards, *The Great Awakening* (London: Banner of Truth Trust, 1976), 215.

10. Helmut Thielicke, *The Silence of God* (Grand Rapids, Mich.: William B. Eerdmans Publishing Co., 1962), 14-5.

11. Charles Haddon Spurgeon in *The Shadow of the Broad Brim*, by Richard E. Day (Valley Forge: Judson Press, 1934), 177-8.

12. George MacDonald, "Lost and Found" in *Anthology of Jesus*, ed. Warren W. Wiersbe (Grand Rapids, Mich.: Kregel Publications, 1981), 129.

13. Henri Nouwen, *In the Name of Jesus* (New York: The Crossroad Publishing Co., 1993), 38.

14. C.S. Lewis, *The Weight of Glory and Other Addresses* (Grand Rapids, Mich.: Eerdmans, 1965), 1-2.

15. C.S. Lewis, quoted in *Renewing America's Soul*, by Howard E. Butt, Jr. (New York: The Continuum Publishing Co., 1996), 1.

16. Chambers, *My Utmost for His Highest*, 2.

17. George MacDonald, *Creation in Christ*, ed. Rolland Hein (Wheaton, Ill.: Harold Shaw Publishers, 1976), 281.

18. A. W. Tozer, *The Knowledge of the Holy* (New York: Harper & Row Publishers, 1961), 121.